WITHDRAWN

China Clipper

China
Clipper

by

Ronald W. Jackson

EVEREST HOUSE
Publishers   *New York*

The author wishes to thank *The New York Times* for permission to
reprint its front page of March 15, 1935.

For Marcy

Contents

Contents

Foreword

WHEN I BEGAN THIS STORY, years ago, it centered on the exploits of the legendary flying boat, the China Clipper and on Captain Edwin Musick, Pan American's premier and world-famous pilot of the 1930s. The story is now very different but it remained in this original version until late in the game. What has bubbled to the top is the story of the Hawaii Clipper's last flight to the Far East and the ponderous circumstances which made that one flight different from all of the others.

I suppose authors usually can point to something that triggered the idea for their books. I cannot. I was born long after the trans-Pacific Clippers first flew to China and even after the China Clipper made its last commercial flight. So I have no residual compulsion to call up this story. I could go into some detail about this but, in short, this story is not in any way part of my past. I don't even know where or how I first stumbled on this idea or where I first heard the name China Clipper. I only recall that one morning I decided to write about this flying boat. Well, I did not write about the China Clipper to any real degree but what I did find was another story which is far more intriguing and which is filled with convoluted facts that take off in one direction or another but come back *always* to the same story. Tracking this story down took years and the time was filled with finding contradicting facts, hitting dead ends, false leads, and frustration. In the end there were surprises and possibilities which I had never imagined when I first began. When I finally began to concentrate more and more on the Hawaii Clipper's last flight, the story broke very quickly and I remember more than once saying out loud to myself, "I don't believe it." Now, I do believe it.

Upon first glance *China Clipper* will appear to be two stories, the adventure of the Hawaii Clipper's last flight and another rooted in the history of the Pacific and how Pan American developed the Pacific air route to China. They are really the same, though. What I eventually realized was that the Hawaii Clipper's flight crystalized all that had preceded it and that its fate was a product of all that surrounded it. I did not even consider blending these two story lines until I was well into my third year on *China Clipper*. I have learned that stories, even nonfiction, do not arrive full blown, they evolve. It took months to sort out the information I found and more time to begin the tedious process of placing one bit of information next to another. It took still more time to think about that construction, discard it, place another piece of information in the same position and then perhaps begin again. And not only has it taken time but it has taken the idle mind, the subconscious, to put the pieces together. And then on top of all of this I had to live with images of people I never knew, from a past I did not live, to put all of this together. A writer, I have found, never escapes his work. Never.

But before any of this piecing took place I needed real information. The broadest outline of *China Clipper* was found in old newspaper and magazine articles and in scores, even hundreds of books. But the real core of *China Clipper* was built on information from original sources I found for the most part in Pan American's New York Archives and in the National Archives in Washington, D.C. The initial research did not take long—perhaps four months—but dredging up hidden pieces of the story which brought it to its final form took years of patience, phone calls, additional reading, waiting, revising, and interviews. One aspect of this story—the incidents of sabotage—eluded me for most of the four years and even now they are not complete. The story of these incidents proved especially elusive primarily because many simply refused to talk or cautiously denied that they occurred. So, finally I was forced to build a composite of what I believe really occurred. First the sabotage incidents are based on the oral confirmation by two men and one woman who said that they personally knew or had heard about these incidents. They are also based on FBI reports which took three years to obtain by the Freedom of Information Act, on letters from the National Archives, on news clippings and from reports found in Pan American Archives. The outline of these events is accurate but because all of these sources abruptly end—even the FBI reports—the specifics are debatable. Part of the reason for this is, of course, the forty plus years since these events occurred. I also believe some government documents have been lost over the years and that some, for reasons unclear, will not openly discuss this subject.

There is also an intuitive side of *China Clipper*, an aspect not easily explained. For instance, I have never flown aboard a flying boat, I have not visited Midway or Guam, I do not know how to fly an airplane, nor have I spoken to the principal characters simply because most are dead. So there were times that I became part of the story. I have flown many times, seen seaplanes take-off and land. I lived in Hawaii, landed at Wake. I rummaged through reams of old magazines to get a sense of the era and talked to anyone I could find who had seen, ridden in, or had anything to say about these giant flying boats. I studied every aspect of the trans-Pacific flights. I found out what time the Hawaii Clipper took off each day, found out when the sun set, I looked to see what the newspapers were reporting in July 1938, what movies were playing. I thought about the people aboard the Hawaii Clipper constantly. I even dreamt about flying in the Clippers and some fragments of those dreams appear here. More than once, the weight of all of this overwhelmed me and I am sure that some of that anxiety found its way into parts of this story. It all came into play.

There is a line, for example, in which Wah Sun Choy says, "You don't ask for nothing, you don't get nothing." A Chinese waiter at Trader Vic's said that to a friend when asked if salad came with dinner. The personality that line revealed fit with what I knew about Wah Sun Choy, so I used it. As I said, the framework is accurate, but the specifics are open to debate. The conversations and incidents which take place aboard the Hawaii Clipper and some of the finer aspects of the sabotage scenes are manufactured but they like the rest of *China Clipper* are based on hard facts culled from State and Navy Department letters, memoranda of conversations, from company brochures, newsletters, accident reports, Congressional records, interviews, and hundreds of sources altogether.

There was also a mood about those six-day flights to China. I think it is here and for one passenger, Wah Sun Choy, I am sure the journey must have been bittersweet.

Introduction

In November 1935, Pan American Airways' legendary flying boat, the China Clipper, inaugurated trans-Pacific commercial flights to the Far East. It was an event that immediately captured the attention and the imagination of the world. While the country was wracked by depression and hopelessness, Pan Am's flying boats transported millions into a world of armchair adventure. Immediately, a mythology began to embrace the giant flying boats—they were the stuff dreams were made of. Hundreds of magazine and newspaper articles chronicled the six-day flights across the Pacific, enterprising restaurant owners changed the names of their establishments to "China Clipper," laundries did the same, and a comical dance called "China Clipper" was introduced in the late 1930s. Even Warner Brothers in Hollywood capitalized on the country's enthusiasm by producing a fictionalized version of Pan Am's exploits in the Pacific entitled *China*

Clipper, starring Humphrey Bogart and Pat O'Brien.

There was, however, a lot more to the trans-Pacific flights than the floss of comical dances and movies. In the guise of commercial development the trans-Pacific line was really the first stage of preparation for World War II.

In the 1930s the political stability of the Pacific was already collapsing and the United States navy found itself dangerously vulnerable in the Pacific. Through a popular policy of isolationism and treaty limitation, the United States had only the most feeble, widely scattered defenses in the Pacific while Japan was actively building a formidable war machine.

But when Pan American announced that it planned to fly the Pacific, the navy instantly knew, after years of frustration, that this was the ruse it needed to fortify the Pacific. By 1938, the trans-Pacific line was well established and the Clippers were making weekly flights from San Francisco to China via the strategically vital route through Pearl Harbor, Midway, Wake, Guam, and Manila.

In July 1938, on the eve of the Second World War, one of Pan Am's flying boats, the Hawaii Clipper, departed San Francisco with twelve passengers and a crew of nine. By all appearances, the flight was identical to the 228 flights that had preceded it. But it was not the same. The Hawaii Clipper was flying into the focal point of all the forces that were conspiring to begin the coming war.

This then is the story of a twenty-six-ton flying boat bound for China—and the military confrontations, acts of espionage, political forces, and sabotage that surrounded this flight.

Ronald W. Jackson

China Clipper

1

Alameda on San Francisco Bay

July 23, 1938

SITTING ON A HARD WOODEN BENCH in Pan American's waiting room, Wah Sun Choy gently tugged on his right shirt cuff and then on his left so that they covered his wrists. Choy did this from time to time to calm himself. It was a nervous habit of such little consequence, though, that neither Choy nor any of his friends had ever really noticed the frequency of the ritual.

Twelve passengers were packed cheek to jowl in the tiny waiting room. Choy surveyed his fellow travelers, dabbing a bead of perspiration as it trickled down his forehead. Then in one sweeping motion he mopped his brow to forestall a reoccurrence of the embarrassment. It was just 2:45 P.M. Time and space seemed to be closing in on Choy.

The crowded room detonated his nervousness as did the thought of the six-day flight to China. In a futile effort to assuage his uneasiness he reached for the copy of the San Francisco *Examiner* he had tucked under his leg.

He skimmed the headlines: *Russians Battle Jap Allies, New Dealer Hints Roosevelt Plans to Seek 3d Term, Crazed Mother Slays 2 Children and Herself.* Choy shook the paper and folded back the front page. A small three-paragraph article on page two hit home:

STUBBORN CHINESE FIGHT TO DEATH

With backing from land, air, and sea bombardment the Japanese army had launched a fierce assault on the Lion Hill Fort near Kiukiang which threatened to force the Nationalists that much deeper into China. Clearly, China's war with Japan was failing. In his heart Wah Sun Choy expected this sort of news. It was not surprising.

For months Choy had eagerly anticipated this trip, but now a sense of dread rushed through his gut. Pacific politics were at the flash point and there were certain risks in flying to China now. The fighting around Kiukiang was only the most recent example of the dangers in and around China. For seven years Japan had feasted upon the flesh of China—first smashing Manchuria in 1931 and in 1937 invading Peking, burning Shanghai, raping Nanking, and bombing Canton. Now desperately reaching for the elusive victory, Japan had grasped China in a stranglehold designed to squeeze the life out of the country. Since spring Japan had maintained an effective two-thousand-mile land and sea blockade, which had sharply cut the flow of supplies and money into China. The blockade was not impenetrable though.

Pan American Airways' three trans-Pacific Clippers pierced the blockade at Macao, and though the flights carried little physical support, they were an important psychological connection with the West. While the United States labeled the line "commercial," Japan saw the weekly flights to China as a direct challenge to its military power. America's isolationist policy in the Pacific was an illusion and Japan knew it.

From Hawaii to Manila, from the Aleutians to Samoa, America had been entrenched in the Pacific Ocean for decades. Pan American's Clipper bases at Hawaii, Midway, Wake, Guam, and the Philippines—islands that had long been considered remote—extended America's frontier to the doorstep of China. Few Americans fathomed the military implications of the trans-Pacific air route, but on the other side of the Pacific Japan saw very clearly that the Pan American line bisected its own highly strategic islands in Micronesia. Japan had tolerated the Pacific flights to Hong Kong and Macao for nearly three years; but in 1938 it decided that the flights compromised the success of the blockade.

Earlier in the year the Japanese vice minister for foreign affairs, Kenosuke Horinouchi, forwarded a carefully worded dispatch to the American ambassador to Japan, Joseph Grew, asking that the United States stop the Clipper flights into Macao:

> . . . According to most recent reports received by the Japanese government, Chinese airplanes are frequently active in the vicinity of Canton, and consequently, the Japanese Navy cannot neglect preparations for ordinary offensive operations. British airplanes in Hong Kong are for the present refraining from flying over the vicinity of the Manshan Islands. In view of the possibility that, due to flights over such area by airplanes of the Pan American Airways, some unfortunate error involving the Japanese Navy might occur, I have the honor to request that measures be urgently taken with a view to flights over the Manshan Islands not to be undertaken for the time being.

The United States refused to recognize this request because it violated the principle of the freedom of the seas, but Pan American took the warning seriously enough to fly into Macao only when the seas around south China were clear of all military activity. The blockade was a clear-cut threat, but there was another far more insidious danger which was more difficult to confront. In late June through early July, Acting Secretary of Commerce Colonel J. Monroe Johnson had heard rumors that one of the Clippers might soon be sabotaged. The talk had been vague and the rumors died down, but the fear of a potential disaster lingered with Johnson through late July.

Secretary Johnson was among the very few who had heard these rumors; certainly those flying aboard the Clippers knew nothing about them. On July 23 the China Clipper, the most famous of Pan Am's Pacific flying boats, was inbound from Hong Kong, the Philippine Clipper was en route to the Far East, and at 3:00 P.M. the Hawaii Clipper, Flight 229, was scheduled to be off for the Orient.

Wah Sun Choy planned to visit his mother and sister in Hong Kong and if things worked the way he planned, see his brother, Frank, who was flying a fighter on the northern Chinese war front. But as Choy was about to board the Hawaii Clipper he could not help worrying about the real purpose of his trip: the delivery of the $3 million to Chiang Kai-shek. Choy felt tired, let-down, and his concern about safely delivering the money to Chungking, the Nationalist capital, sapped his enthusiasm for the flight. The six-day trip to China should have been one of the high points in his life; he had dreamt about it since the line opened and he had worked hard for it.

The wealthy president of a small Jersey City-based corporation, Wah Sun Choy owned three restaurants. Two were located at Jersey City's Journal Square, the Plaza Tea

Garden and the China Clipper Cafe, and one at 3 Doyers Street in Manhattan also called China Clipper. Choy was so enamored with the trans-Pacific flying boats that he had decorated his two Clipper restaurants with photographs of the China Clipper. In addition to overseeing the restaurants, Choy had put in long hours over the past year working to bolster the sagging Nationalist war effort against Japan by serving as the chairman of the Chinese War Relief Committee. Through a series of social events—mainly dinners, called rice bowl parties—Choy helped raise the $3 million safely tucked aboard the Hawaii Clipper. All of this, the romance of the trans-Pacific Clippers, the anticipated adventure of the flight, the unending work for the Relief Committee and the opportunity to help China fueled his child-like excitement for this trip.

Choy's buoyancy was contagious and on Wednesday, the night before he flew to San Francisco, his friends threw a lavish bon voyage party for him at the Plaza Tea Garden. Everyone had a grand time. There was plenty to eat and drink but underlying the false cheer everyone knew that the $3 million would not turn the tide against Japan—only direct backing from the United States could do that.

As Choy looked about at his eleven fellow passengers in the small, white waiting room, he thought with some bitterness that they, like the United States, were just going about their own business.

Of the twelve about to board six were flying only as far as Honolulu. One of those, Henry Huntington, a St. Louis manufacturer, was racing to the bedside of his brother, who had collapsed shortly after arriving in Honolulu on the previous flight of the China Clipper. Traveling with Huntington was Dr. Fred Reichert, a San Francisco surgeon, who had been engaged to perform emergency brain surgery on Huntington's brother immediately after their arrival in Honolulu. Homer Orvis, an executive with the Cotton Exchange in New

York; Eric Nelson, a New York mechanical engineer; and Marvin Murphy, an executive from Philadelphia, were flying to Hawaii on business. Darwin Teihet, advertising director for the Hawaii Pineapple Company, had just completed business on the mainland and was on his way home.

Rudely, Choy was shaken from his thoughts when a bell from a speaker directly above his head rang once and a voice announced, "The crew will board." Embarrassed with the way he jumped when the bell sounded Choy smiled at Kenneth Kennedy sitting next to him. Kennedy, one of the six scheduled to fly to China, was Pan Am's Pacific Division traffic manager and had made this flight many times over the years. As traffic manager Kennedy was charged with making periodic trips across the Pacific to check on ticketing, marketing, and the general health of the Pacific operation. Kennedy had worked for Pan Am since 1935. After fighting in France during the First World War Kennedy temporarily went into banking, and then, in the early 1930s, moved into aviation with the Boeing School of Aeronautics. Following this he became United Airlines' traffic manager. When the Pacific route opened he eagerly snapped up the opportunity to join Pan Am.

This morning Kennedy's wife, Marjorie, had driven down to the Alameda Pan Am base from their home in the Oakland hills. Unlike the others waiting to board the Hawaii Clipper, Kennedy was not excited about the trip; the flight was just part of his job. Rather, Kennedy was more concerned about a recent notice he had received telling him that Oakland planned to build a new freeway down Mountain Boulevard and that they would have to vacate their house shortly.

Some minutes after the crew boarded the bell rang twice and the same voice announced, "Passengers for the Hawaii Clipper will please board." One by one the twelve men stood up and filed through the narrow door to the pier. At the end of the dock the men waited near the tail of the Clipper until their names were called. When Ivan Parker, the ship's steward, called their names they stepped up a set of metal stairs to the top of the hull and then descended into the flying boat.

Numbered NC–14714, the Hawaii Clipper was the third of three flying boats built by Glenn L. Martin at his Middle River, Maryland plant and used by Pan American in the Pacific. Though each of the three Clippers had its own personality and individual quirks, each was identical in appearance; not even the pilots who flew them regularly could tell one from the other without looking at the name painted on the bow.

Sleek, forward-looking in a manner unlike any other flying boats, the Martin Clippers were the sum of the most advanced technology of the era, the product of the finest engineering talent in the United States. They were the largest successful heavier-than-air aircraft, the culmination of nearly three years of planning and construction. And they were more than good-looking machines; they were rugged and capable of withstanding the worst.

Traditionally, flying boats had been awkward, uninspired aircraft dutifully making their rounds over the world's seaways. But the Martin flying boats changed the dated image. They were an uncompromising leap forward in aeronautical technology. The genius of dozens of engineers blended the stalwart lines of a heavy duty seaplane with the polished airiness of modern design. Aerodynamics and streamlining led the way in 1930s design of everything from ashtrays to belt buckles, from skyscrapers to toasters reflected this and the Clippers were the living symbol of this look into the future. The Hawaii Clipper resting on San Francisco Bay embodied all of the modern values—it was long, low, fast, and easy on the eye.

None of this came easily. Before the ships reached construction, months of planning and detail work went into the design of the flying boats. Months were spent in preliminary wind-tunnel testing to produce an efficient wing/hull relationship which would allow the Clippers to rise easily from the water. Following wind-testing, water-tank tests were conducted to perfect a hull contour, which would give the giant boat stability in rough open seas while maintaining the capability of quick, efficient take-offs. Specialists in structural steel design made thousands of computations to determine the greatest strengths that could be attained from the conflicting requirements of external aerodynamic streamlining and internal bracing.

Taking a note from paper-box manufacturers, designers corrugated part of the upper hull to achieve maximum strength with minimum weight. Borrowing from shipbuilders, the Martin engineers designed the Clippers with double bottoms to help prevent sinking if the hull were damaged.

Instead of cumbersome and structurally dangerous wing pontoons, large seawings or sponsons extended from the hull at the waterline and gave the Clipper unusually good stability in the water. Although primarily designed to keep the flying boat on an even keel, the sponsons served triple duty by also holding 1,900 gallons of gasoline and generating additional lift once the ship was airborne.

All of this produced a 26-ton flying boat which was the first aircraft in the world sufficiently powerful to carry the equivalent of its weight as payload. This was a remarkable advance which meant that the Clipper was the only aircraft in the world that could carry enough fuel in addition to passengers and freight to make the long Pacific hauls. When fully loaded the Martin Clipper could fly an astounding 3,200 miles non-stop at 130 miles per hour. It was something no other aircraft could duplicate. It was beyond belief.

To most passengers this information was meaningless; what they noticed and cared about was that the Martin flying boats were comfortable. While still in the design stage engineers produced a full-scale model of the interior so they could study the position of control cables, wiring, plumbing, and structural supports in relation to the most comfortable seating arrangement. Once the interior had been designed, the passenger compartments were soundproofed to allow conversation at normal levels. The blue and green colors used in the sixteen-foot lounge were coordinated in a harmonious, relaxing scheme.

In the design and construction of the three flying boats Martin also built in every known backup system and safety device. The Martin engineers, with input from Pan American, designed six watertight compartments into the Clipper's ninety-foot hull so that if a Clipper were damaged and forced down at sea, any two compartments could keep it afloat—even in moderately rough seas. Two main radios were carried; if both failed, a small emergency set was available along with a trailing antenna.

Also in case a Clipper were forced down each carried flares, an auxiliary generator, rubber life rafts, concentrated foods, canned water, condensed milk, even a salt-water still. Shotguns, fishing bait and tackle were stored in the emergency locker. In all there were enough supplies to sustain fifteen lives aboard the Clipper or in a life raft for ninety days. But the chances of a disaster or some mechanical failure were incalculably small. The Clippers' engines were the best in the world.

In 1935, Martin originally equipped the Clippers with four Pratt & Whitney twin row Wasp engines. Each fourteen-cylinder engine was geared, supercharged, and fitted with a Hamilton Standard Constant Speed Propeller to produce 800 horsepower. Just a few months prior to Flight 229, Pan Am refitted the three Clippers with new 950-h.p. Pratt & Whitney engines and new Hamilton Hydromatic Propellers. Any two engines could keep a Clipper aloft.

All in all, the Martin Clipper was, quite simply, the finest aeronautical product to date.

Choy looked out of his window at the white caps on the bay. Though he was warm it was really unseasonably cool, just 60 degrees. The usual afternoon wind was building, blowing the afternoon fog through the Golden Gate. Choy leaned his head on the bulkhead directly behind his seat trying to steady the quivering muscles in his neck. It was no use, it would not be the relaxing trip he had planned. The troubles in the Far East were much too serious to even temporarily displace with some romantic notions about the trans-Pacific Clippers.

2
Take-off

July 23, 1938

O N THE BRIDGE OF THE HAWAII CLIPPER, Captain Leo Terletsky fired up the engines. First the outboard engine on the left wing sputtered and coughed blue smoke across the water. A moment later the outboard engine on the right wing came to life, quickly followed by the two inboard engines. Terletsky idled the engines while he waited for the all-clear signal from a launch searching for debris in the bay which could damage the Clipper's hull on take-off.

Terletsky was a better-than-average pilot, but among those within Pan American, he was considered only average. This was because Pan Am had strict, uncommonly high standards for its flight personnel. So anyone within the ranks of Pan Am was automatically counted among the best. Terletsky served well but he did not have the spark of leadership that would help him rank higher in the eyes of his peers. Born in

Russia, he was more formal and distant than other Clipper pilots. Some interpreted his solemnity as arrogance, others saw him as merely quiet, almost deferential. Everyone agreed, though, that Terletsky had a firm manner and never raised his voice in anger.

Terletsky had fought in the Russian Revolution, but when the tide turned strongly in favor of the communists he fled to the United States. After arriving, he attended Columbia University. Later he learned how to fly at a Curtiss-Wright school on Long Island. Through the early 1920s he eked out a living barnstorming in New England, then bounced from Waco Aircraft to Barrett Airways to Maughton Aviation Company until he joined Pan American in 1936.

In order to become a pilot for Pan Am, Terletsky, like all of the airline's pilots, had to meet rigorous qualifications which far exceeded what was required by the domestic airlines. Starting at the lowest rung an Apprentice Pilot worked throughout Pan Am's system learning all the phases of flying, including the communications, traffic, and mechanical departments. From the apprentice level the pilots were promoted to Junior Pilot, but only after they had been licensed in radio operation and mechanics and proved they understood the principles of celestial navigation. Pan Am also encouraged the pilots to learn a foreign language and something about international law. As junior pilots the men often flew aboard the Clippers as flight engineers. Here they learned the intricacies of the Clippers in flight by watching over the dials and instruments that monitored the four powerful engines. Once they mastered all of this they were finally promoted to Senior Pilot. Further, in order to fly as a captain in the Pacific a pilot needed to fly a minimum of two thousand hours for the airline and make five trips to China before he could take command of a Clipper.

Now forty-three and living with his wife in Palo Alto,

thirty-five miles south of San Francisco, Terletsky exceeded the standards for captain. In the same minute detail as his log book, Terletsky's thin, hard face verified that he had accumulated over 9,200 hours' total flight time, with 1,600 over the Pacific. Though he was not the best aviator on the line he was generally considered Pan Am's best "sailor."

Once the flying boats were freed from their moorings, handling them was more like sailing a large yacht than controlling an airplane. Subject to the whims of currents, waves and wind, the flying boats drifted dangerously unless they were expertly controlled. Better than anyone else, Terletsky knew how to use the engines and wing flaps to "sail" the Clippers precisely where he wanted them to go.

Like all of Pan Am's pilots, he knew well the dangers of the Pacific storm season and the unique handling characteristics of the Martin Clippers. They could fly into a thirty-, forty-, or perhaps even a fifty-mile-per-hour head wind, but not much more than that. Low cloud cover, fog, and rain all generated additional dangers in the air. There were dozens of other factors besides the weather that might affect the flights to the Orient. Terletsky was fully aware of the problems of a sticky fuel pump, a faulty magneto, low oil pressure, or the sure disaster that freak structural failure meant. The list of potential failures might well have continued to cover every conceivable part, pump, cable, piece of tubing, structural support, weather aberration—and then embrace all the causes of disaster that were not yet fully understood or discovered.

Terletsky also knew that his success or failure, as for every aviator, ultimately came down to being in the right place at the right time. Why should an engine fail while he was flying and not someone else? There was no reason for it, and by the same token there was every reason for it to happen to him. Failures such as these were beyond Terletsky's control; they were problems in the realm of incalculable mathematical probabilities—chance, fate. His only hedge against being in the wrong place was to cut the odds for disaster by leaving as little to chance as possible. In the last analysis, he knew that his duty was ordained by his instincts and experience, and that his fate was determined by the unknown.

Just a few minutes past 3:00 P.M., Terletsky sailed the Hawaii Clipper into the open waters of San Francisco Bay. Pointing the nose of the Clipper toward the Oakland-San Francisco Bridge and the prevailing wind from the Golden Gate, he pushed a power signal-button on the instrument panel. Above him, in the engineer's cabin, a light flashed "Full Power."

The four engines began to whine, sending the sweet scent of creosote and gasoline exhaust over the bay. At first moving slowly through the chilly water, within seconds the Clipper was dancing across the bay at sixty miles per hour.

Looking out the square window, Choy watched the corrugated sponsons etch a deep continuous pattern on the water's surface. Suddenly, the ship's vibration smoothed to a deep-throated hum as it hopped from one swell to the next. White salt spray shot past the windows. Once again the Hawaii Clipper smacked into a whitecap and then, without apparent effort, the ship gently rocked back and left the bay just a few feet below. "We're up," someone shouted. "I timed it at forty-five seconds."

The heavy-set, balding man who timed the take-off was Howard French. A prosperous automobile dealer from Portland, Oregon, French was the only passenger traveling on vacation. And this was unusual. Since a one-way ticket to Honolulu was $360 and the fare to Hong Kong $800, few casual travelers were able to afford to fly the Pacific simply for pleasure. But French was easily wealthy enough to pay $1,600 for the trip to China and back.

Overweight and balding, French was well known and somewhat influential in the Portland area. In addition to his automotive business, he was the commanding officer of the 321st Observation Squadron in the Pacific Northwest. After graduating from Washington State College, French learned to fly when he joined the army. During his active military career, he fought in the Mexican border disputes and later in France where he was shot down twice. After the war, with the rank of major, he joined the 321st.

A few days earlier, on Thursday, while French was picking up his United Airlines ticket to San Francisco at the downtown American Express office, some friends from the Portland Police Department playfully arrested him and put him in a paddy wagon. With the siren wailing across town French, always up for a good joke, yelled out the back window that he was being kidnapped. At the airport, the police escorted him up to the Douglas airliner. French played along, yelling and screaming as his friends carried him aboard. He loved the attention and with a hearty wave he told them, "I want to be in Canton when the Japs pull another raid on the town."

Already Second Officer George Davis was walking through the passenger lounge, checking for damage that might have occurred to the hull or the wing struts from the water forces. As usual nothing was found, but it was part of the required precautionary procedure the second officer performed immediately after every take-off. Climbing at an even but slow rate, the Clipper turned west around Coit Tower on Telegraph Hill and skirted the northern shoreline of San Francisco . At Point Bonita, land's end, Terletsky called, "Five hundred feet." Directly below, white fog was pouring in through the Golden Gate, spreading out like a deep, downy canopy up and down the coast. On Choy's side the sun-baked Marin Headlands were easing past the windows; on the other side San Francisco's packed mass of buildings was already receding into the haze that hung over the city. Choy pressed his face against the window and for nearly five minutes watched the coast as it dissolved into a thin gray line at the horizon.

When the Clipper marked nine thousand feet, normal cruising altitude, Terletsky signaled Harold Cox, the engineer, "Cruising Speed." For a moment it seemed as though the engines had gone out of synchronization as the power was cut and the pitch of the propellers was readjusted for the altitude and the new power setting. A moment later the engines quieted to an even purr. At 125 miles per hour, the noise and excitement of the take-off subsided.

The sudden silence after the roar of the take-off always caught the passengers by surprise. The Clipper seemed to hang motionless above the light-speckled Pacific, and for the first time since take-off, the men looked about the ship. Choy and French were smiling. The thrill of becoming airborne and the intimacy of the lounge created a sort of instant bond of camaraderie among the passengers.

Choy had already spoken to Kennedy and French but he had not yet said anything to the other three men flying to China. Sitting across the lounge from Choy, Edward Wyman thumbed through a magazine. He had not yet introduced himself. Formerly an assistant to Juan Trippe, president of Pan American, Wyman was well known on the business side of aviation and had at least a nodding acquaintance with Pan Am official Kennedy. Wyman lived in Bronxville, New York, with his wife and two children, and was now vice-president of export sales for Curtiss-Wright. Handsome in a classic manner, he was beginning an around-the-world sales trip.

The other two flying to China, Dr. Fred Meier and Dr. Earl McKinley, were engaged in a private conversation. Personal friends as well as colleagues, they were traveling together on a grant supplied by the National Research

Council. Meier, from Chevy Chase, Maryland, was a senior scientist for the Department of Agriculture. For nearly ten years he had been working on a theory that micro-organisms were spread throughout the world on the upper-air currents of the atmosphere. The purpose of his trip was to take air samples over the Pacific with a device he invented called the "Air Hook." McKinley planned to help Meier with the experiment but as the dean of the Medical School at George Washington University in Washington, D.C., and a leprosy expert, he was intent on working on his own experiments at the Culion Leprosy Colony in the Philippines and later Hong Kong.

Fifty miles out of San Francisco, Steward Parker served tea, coffee, chocolate, and small cakes on the dining table. Life on the Clippers progressed at a pleasant, well-ordered pace. In the summer, by the sixth hour of the flight, night came. Through the afternoon a fertile blue belt of air and water circled the ship; now, just over 750 miles out of San Francisco, the sun was setting. In the span of a half hour the blue sky lightened to yellow, then sparkled with bright reds and oranges. Just before dark, the sky deepened to a rich purple. Above, the long wispy summer clouds turned pink, then vanished in the night as the first stars began to shine. Under the right wing the moon appeared. Within moments it seemed as though the Hawaii Clipper were flying into an impenetrable blackness. Only the moon and the long blue exhaust flames from each engine lighted the night.

Parker walked through the ship snapping on the small shaded lamps on the bulkheads. Each change in the day brought about a change in mood. Dark set the passengers on edge, making each feel lonely and vulnerable in the black void around them. Parker, making his twenty-sixth trip across the Pacific, was familiar with the phenomenon, and he picked this moment to pass out the dinner menu, bringing the passengers back to the secure comfort of the Clipper.

While some continued to sip tea, others resumed their momentarily interrupted conversation. Parker spread out a white tablecloth and placed heavy water goblets, china, and silver at six settings. With twelve aboard, he would have to serve two separate dinner seatings.

Tonight dinner was the usual simple but satisfying fare: clear consommé, salad, chicken fricassee, vegetables, and cake. During the second seating, Parker went aft and began making up the berths. After dinner, Parker informed each of the men individually that his berth had been made up and that they could expect to land in Pearl Harbor at 7:30 A.M. local time. By 10:30 everyone retired except Choy.

Choy enjoyed playing with words. For amusement he asked his friends to call him "Watson" instead of "Wah Sun." He also wrote small poems for himself. For nearly an hour he tried to form mental images of the day—the water splashing past the window, the roar of the engines, the setting sun. But he was too tired to write anything. Near midnight Parker suggested that Choy retire.

Before leaving the lounge the two talked for a moment. They chatted easily about the restaurant business and all of the problems of satisfying different tastes but when Choy asked Parker about his work, Parker's tone seemed bitter. He confided that he had become a steward only so that he could move into the radio division, his first love. At thirty-seven, Parker was ambitious but he knew that the move into radio was unlikely. He told Choy that he had just been offered the chance to become the manager of the Pan Am hotel on Guam, an opportunity he said he planned to accept. The career advancement pleased him. But what he did not tell Choy was that his work was ruining his marriage.

Parker's wife, Ruth, lived in Los Angeles and was not at

all happy with her husband's long trips away from home. Recently, Parker had started spending his time off between flights in the San Francisco area, and he had not seen Ruth for nearly seven months. The upcoming promotion had strained the marriage to the breaking point; Ruth flatly refused to move to Guam. So unknown to Ruth, Parker had just filed for a divorce. What he did not know was that Ruth had reconsidered and decided to go to Guam after all.

Parker showed Choy to his lower berth, and as he turned back the covers he pointed out that they used yellow sheets to help prevent air sickness. When Choy asked how the sheets did this, Parker was unable to give him an answer. It was just what he had been told, Parker said. There was no reason to worry about airsickness tonight, though; the sky was calm, the Clipper was steady.

Choy glanced out the window near his pillow. The moon still hung near the wing. He tried to think of some words to describe it but he couldn't.

Terletsky had been at the controls for nearly nine hours, with only short breaks for dinner and coffee. His first officer, co-pilot Mark Walker, had just awakened from a nap and came up to the bridge to relieve Terletsky.

This hour of the flight was like a dream. Only the dull glow of the radium dials lit the bridge. The passengers were asleep and except for the steady comforting roar of the engines the night was quiet. Terletsky's body hummed comfortably with fatigue. Walker's voice broke the spell. "Take over, Captain?" Walker was a good pilot, better than most and perhaps from a technical point of view, better than Terletsky.

Walker and the rest of the crew represented the Pan American ideal. Every man in the nine-man crew had years of experience on the ground and in the air, and as the company preferred, most were navy trained. Walker, a reserve ensign, had 1,900 hours' flying time with 1,575 over the Pacific; he had learned to fly at the naval air station in Coronado. Second Officer George Davis, who was now below but would come on the bridge when Terletsky retired, was also navy trained. In a few minutes he would fly in the right seat. Davis was anxious about this flight. His wife was now over eight months pregnant with their first child, and he wanted to get back to California as soon as possible.

Third Officer Jose Sauceda, originally from Texas, now lived with his wife and child on 15th Street in Oakland. Sauceda, though not navy trained, had been with Pan American since June 1929. Fourth Officer John Jewett had more total flying time than Sauceda, but since he had less time over the Pacific, he was the junior pilot on the flight. Jewett, just twenty-seven, had graduated from M.I.T. with a B.S. in science, then learned to fly in the navy. Before PAA hired him in 1936, he had worked for Douglas Aircraft's engineering department.

Radio Officer William McCarty, thirty-three, looked very much like a young Jack Dempsey. One of the better-qualified radio operators in the Pacific, McCarty had worked aboard the luxury liner *Lurline* until he joined Pan American.

Above the bridge in the engineer's cabin, the point where the hull and the wings met, Flight Engineer Howard Cox watched over the four engines. Around him were over 180 dials and levers that monitored and controlled the giant ship's engines. Occasionally, as a matter of personal habit, Cox would poke a flashlight through the window on each side of the cabin to visually check each engine.

Cox had spent the last few weeks in Seattle acting as Pan Am's technical advisor on the development of a new generation of flying boats being built by Boeing. He had been scheduled to go back to New York, but troubles interrupted the PAA schedule so Cox was temporarily assigned to the Hawaii Clipper. Working with Cox was Thomas Tatum. Tatum, twenty-nine, had worked as a ground mechanic for Pan Am on Midway, Wake, and Guam; this was his first flight. Cox was breaking him in. All in all, it was a well-trained, highly experienced crew. With the benevolent summer weather ahead it was going to be a better-than-average flight, Terletsky thought as Davis relieved him.

3

Pacific Perspective

1852-1923

*E*ARLY IN THE NINETEENTH CENTURY the discovery of guano, bird droppings, an important and highly effective fertilizer, opened the Pacific as America's new frontier. This discovery led to the passage of the Guano Act in 1856, then to increased exploration of the Pacific and finally by the mid-1930s to the creation of Pan American's Clipper bases. The Guano Act played such an important role in the development of the Pacific because it stipulated that any island that had not already been claimed by another country and that had been mined by Americans for its guano deposits could, at the discretion of the President, be considered part of the United States. By 1880, of the hundreds of atolls discovered in the South Pacific, some fifty fell under the Guano Act and hence American sovereignty. The small, barren islands in the Line and Phoenix groups, including Baker, Jarvis and Howland, lying approximately halfway between Hawaii and New Zealand, were the ones most heavily mined and soon became known casually, and on some British maps formally, as American Polynesia.

Above the equator American exploration led to the claim of Midway, the northwesternmost atoll of the Hawaiian chain, in 1867. In 1898, as spoils of the Spanish-American War, both Guam and the Philippines became American possessions. Hawaii and Wake were also claimed by the United States in 1898. Finally in 1900 the United States ratified the Berlin Treaty and thus acquired part of Samoa. So, as the twentieth century unfolded, the United States, with island colonies dotting the Pacific, had an abiding interest in the great western ocean.

About the same time, Japan, just emerging from its feudal past, also moved to expand its own Pacific power base. Around 1900, Japan controlled the Kurile islands, which sweep north from Japan to the tip of Kamchatka, as well as part of Sakhalin. Japan also occupied Formosa, the Bonins, which lie south of Tokyo, and the Pescadores, which are huddled near the China coast. So, on the eve of the First World War, the Pacific was neatly but somewhat precariously divided between Germany—which had just purchased the thousands of islands in Micronesia from Spain—Japan, and the United States.

With war surely coming, German domination of a large part of the Pacific was intolerable to Great Britain. Something had to be done. Just months before the war began, Great Britain's foreign secretary, Sir Edward Grey, met with Japanese officials and secretly devised a plan to smash Germany in the Pacific. Literally on the other side of the world, Micronesia was nearly impossible to defend or attack from Europe. So Grey's plan called for Japanese warships to storm Micronesia when the first bomb burst in Europe.

The plan worked well. In August 1914, Japan moved

on the islands and by October, after barely firing a cannon, Japan held all of Micronesia north of the equator. But in his haste to catch Germany off guard, Grey had overlooked an important point, one which would haunt the western allies for the next thirty years. The western Pacific had always been controlled by Europe, and because of its distance from the homeland, Micronesia meant very little in the course of world affairs. Now controlled by an Asian nation, Micronesia was within Japan's logical sphere of influence. Japan's power suddenly rivaled that of the United States, engulfing the Pacific from the southern limits of the Bering Sea to the equator and from the Asian coast to the international date line. Within a mere ninety days after the First World War opened, fully a quarter of the Pacific was made over into a Japanese province.

As early as 1916, the U.S. navy seriously began considering the possibility of a Pacific war with Japan. The Naval Appropriations Bill of that year created the Helm Commission, which was charged with the responsibility of determining the navy's strategic position throughout the world. Much of the commission's report concentrated on the Pacific—specifically on a distant, lonely, almost unheard-of island, Guam.

The Helm Commission's Pacific report worked from a single premise which postulated that sooner or later Congress would grant independence to the Philippines. Without the Philippines and the naval base at Manila, the commission reasoned, it would be impossible to maintain a strong American military stance in the Pacific. Guam, the second westernmost American possession, logically became the next best site from which to defend the western Pacific. With its decision forced upon it by geography, the commission recommended that Guam be converted into a major fleet base. The report was ill-timed because in the following year the United States entered the First World War and money that might have found its way to Guam was appropriated for Europe.

In spite of the European emergency some believed that the Japanese threat in the Pacific demanded immediate attention. In October 1917, Rear Admiral Albert P. Niblack, commander of naval forces at Gibraltar, who also had a distinguished career in the Pacific, wrote the secretary of the navy concerning the now long-abandoned guano islands:

> It is not a question of fortifying, but of providing stepping stones, and lines of communication which may, in case of war, turn out to be lines of operation or which can be converted into such . . . Not all need to be developed, but one of the main considerations is not to leave islands lying around loose. Future generations will not thank us for any carelessness. Our future lies in the Pacific.

Niblack's insights, nearly twenty years ahead of their time, were largely ignored.

The threat of Japanese power in Micronesia remained a secondary problem as long as the war continued, but by 1917 the western allies were forced to come to grips with Japan's claim to Micronesia. The League of Nations decided, rather than grant annexation as Grey had promised, to place the islands under Japan's control as a Class C Mandate. This was close to, but not actually, annexation.

The Mandate meant simply that Japan would have administrative jurisdiction over the islands while the League retained final authority. As dictated, these restrictions prohibited the Japanese from building military bases in Micronesia. For the time being this neutralized western concern that the islands might become a major Pacific fortress.

But what is a military base?

Additions to a harbor or the construction of an airstrip, though ostensibly for commercial purposes, are essentially the same type of facilities the military needs. A harbor built at Kwajalein or Truk for a steamer to transport copra and phosphates to Yokohama serves equally well for a munitions ship. An air base built for commercial transportation is identical to the facilities required by bombing squadrons. The problem of defining a military base asserted itself time and time again in the coming years. Both Japan and the United States deliberately blurred this issue; each used the confusion to secure for itself the greatest possible strategic advantage.

After the war the Joint Board of the Army and Navy as usual once again looked at the Pacific, plotting the most likely course of a war with Japan. Basing many of its conclusions on Japan's possession of Micronesia, the Joint Board's Pacific defense plan by and large followed the Helm Commission's lead of some years earlier. With the bulk of American forces based at Hawaii, the primary objective at the beginning of a war with Japan would be the defense of the Philippines. Here again, the same old problem cropped up. Philippine independence was a coming reality; at best Manila was a temporary base. Beyond that, even if the Philippines were held for a while, the islands were distant, nearly 8,000 miles from California, and the Joint Board estimated that it would take a minimum of seven weeks before the first supplies and reinforcements could reach Manila after a Japanese invasion. By this time, the board conceded, the Philippines would be mortally wounded and rendered indefensible.

The same was true of Guam. Defenseless and sitting alone in the vortex of Micronesia, Guam, if captured, would become the last block in Japan's great Pacific wall. American shipping lanes west of the international date line would be cut, severely protracting the war.

In what was becoming naval policy, the Joint Board in

December 1919 recommended that Guam be developed into a main naval base suitably fortified to defend itself by housing 13,500 men and the Asiatic Fleet. The secretary of the navy, Josephus Daniels, endorsed the board's plan but in the following spring, apparently reacting to growing American isolationism, withdrew his support. Through 1920, the navy continued to lobby for Guam, and in early 1921, success finally seemed assured when the Senate Naval Affairs Committee advised Congress to appropriate funds for fortifying Guam. It failed to pass; the timing was all wrong.

Defeated first because of war and now thwarted because the world was weary of war, Guam seemed fated to remain a lonely American outpost. Some naval officers and senators made a few last desperate attempts to buttress Guam, but the tide had turned—diplomats around the world were already working to reduce fortifications.

Vowing to reduce the number of military bases and control the growth of the world's navies, the Washington Naval Conference opened on Armistice Day 1921. Under the leadership of Great Britain and the United States, the assembled nations fought their way through problem after problem for three months without a concrete treaty. On February 5, 1922, a bargain was struck. In order to stabilize what could become a frantic round of military construction in the Pacific, the United States, Great Britain, and Japan agreed to halt all military building on the Pacific islands; only Hawaii was exempt from this pledge. Hand in hand with the nonbuilding pledge, the three nations decided to control the expansion of the navies by establishing a warship ratio of 5:5:3. Japan was given the smallest ratio but it was not necessarily dealt an inferior position.

Though the United States and Britain seemingly left the conference in a superior position with larger navies, the nonbuilding pledge actually added to Japan's long-term strategic position. Even with nearly twice as many warships as Japan, the nonbuilding provision virtually eliminated any chance of the United States conducting offensive naval warfare in the western Pacific. From a military angle, all American possessions west of Hawaii—Midway, Wake, Guam, Samoa, even Manila—though potentially highly strategic military bases from which the Pacific Fleet could operate, were now no more than desert islands. Japan, on the other hand, was close to Micronesia, Guam, and Manila—so it would be relatively easy for the Imperial navy to conduct an aggressive campaign in China and the western Pacific without interference from the United States.

As far as the navy was concerned the western Pacific was beyond redemption. The Washington Naval Treaty would not expire until December 1936. Not until then, fourteen years later, could the navy begin building defensive facilities west of Hawaii. Estimating that it would take ten years to turn Guam into a first-class base, the navy now assumed that war with Japan between 1922 and 1946 would be tantamount to handing over the western Pacific—Guam, the Philippines, and probably China—to Japan. Still, the treaty did soothe political tensions for a while.

But even this did not last long. On November 13, 1922, the Supreme Court aggravated the settlement by supporting racist exclusion laws, ruling that Japanese were not eligible for U.S. citizenship. And, paralleling America, Japan exhibited similar tendencies of racial superiority and exclusionism. After Japan occupied Micronesia, it instituted a harsh policy of secrecy in the islands, sometimes at the expense of long-time alien residents. Most of the non-native, non-Japanese population was deported from Micronesia, leaving, according to some estimates, only one American in all of the Mandates. Through the 1920s travel by non-Japanese was practically impossible and travel that did occur was under strict guard; by the 1930s alien traffic in Micronesia was impossible. Because of these restrictions and because neither the League of Nations nor the Washington Treaty had taken the precaution of forging an inspection program to oversee Japanese building in Micronesia, U.S. military intelligence about the Mandates was, at best, speculative.

The American military reacted to Japan's secrecy by underwriting a series of intelligence-gathering missions in the early 1920s. The navy's effort was much too timid to discover anything about new Japanese fortifications in Micronesia. In October 1923, the U.S.S. *Milwaukee*, under the command of W. C. Asserson, steamed among the lesser islands in Micronesia, but other than some hydrographic information about reef locations, water depth, and the like, Asserson brought back no substantive intelligence about a military buildup in the western Pacific.

Two years earlier, in 1921, Marine Corps Lieutenant Colonel Earl Hancock Ellis ventured through Micronesia on a highly secret mission. Traveling in the guise of a German trader, Ellis moved through the islands with relative ease for nearly two years. He reported that the islands could indeed present a formidable fortress in the future, but like Asserson, Ellis added little to American intelligence about the Mandates. Not only did the Asserson and Ellis trips provide little new information; they were sloppily managed. Japanese spotters discovered the *Milwaukee* in the Mandates and submitted a strenuous protest to the United States. Ellis suffered more directly. Sometime in 1923 his identity must have been uncovered because on May 12 of that year he died under "mysterious circumstances." He was probably murdered at Koror in the Palaus shortly after his identity was discovered by Japanese officials.

The last Pacific mission, conducted by the U.S. army, began on September 29, 1923. On this date General Billy

Mitchell received orders to survey the Pacific on an overt but nevertheless confidential assignment. Mitchell's report was perhaps the most insightful of all. He diagnosed the Pacific problem roughly in the same manner as had the Helm Commission and the Joint Board. In light of the Washington Treaty, Mitchell saw a bleak future:

All of the white nations look with apprehension at the rising military power of Japan. Japan's total military strength is growing constantly. She is stronger in all ways than she has been in her history. . . . The rumblings of this strife have ceased to be audible whispers, but are loud protests of the Japanese people, the vanguard of the Asiatic. . . . Sooner or later the diplomatic means of handling these questions will fail and a physical means of impressing our will on the hostile state will be the recourse. In other words, war.

Like the Helm Commission and the Joint Board before him Mitchell listed Guam as a primary base. He also included Midway and Wake in his report:

Roughly, Guam lies halfway between Wake Island and Manila, the distance from it to both being about sixteen hundred miles. It is surrounded by the Japanese islands of the Mariana Group. Almost directly to the north of Guam, and at a distance of about one thousand miles, lie the Bonin Islands, connected to Guam by a string of islands whose greatest gap is four hundred miles or four hours flight for the ordinary bombardment airplane. Outside of Japan itself, the Bonin Islands are Japan's strongest position for either offense or defense along the southern line, whether by air or by water. From it, on a radius of about fifteen hundred miles, any force advancing from the United States along the Honolulu-Manila line may be attacked in flank from Wake Island to the Philippines, a distance of over three thousand miles. In case of defeat, the United States forces would have to fall back on their magazines of Manila or Honolulu, both to a flank, or be destroyed, whereas, the Japanese would have their whole base to retire to in case of necessity. . . . From a strategic standpoint, Guam is of the greatest importance.

Mitchell continued, listing the military significance of China, New Guinea, Australia, Singapore, Hong Kong and Java; finally he reminded the army of the great oil reserves in Borneo, Sumatra and Burma and of the tin, rice and rubber of the Malay Peninsula that was so attractive to the resource-poor Japanese. The coming battle would be for all or nothing. Mitchell warned, "There is no use for anyone to question the necessity of white dominance. If the whites do not dominate, then the yellow race will."

4

The Foundation of an Empire

1926-1927

*I*N 1927, when Juan Trippe, president of Pan American, first invested in the airline, he could not possibly have known about the South Pacific expeditions of Asserson, Ellis, or Mitchell, or about the War Department's concern with the increasing power of Japan. Nor could Trippe have imagined that in just a few years Pan American would become the navy's agent in building air bases across the Pacific.

Though Trippe could not have seen these things, the idea should not have surprised him either. Because of massive subsidies from the Post Office Department, Pan American was closely associated with the development of foreign policy from its very first days. Acting as a diplomatic tool, as the official American explorer in Latin America, Pan American proved time and again that it was the right conduit to achieve certain goals on an unofficial basis. By gathering information for government and business, Pan Am had also strengthened its position as a quasi-government agency that had worked quite well with the White House, and with the Post Office, Commerce, and State Departments. With all of this behind Trippe it was only natural to assume that Pan Am could also work with the War Department—after all, Pan American Airways was originally founded not for commercial reasons but to blunt a potential military threat from South America.

In 1920 Dr. Peter Paul von Bauer, a former German pilot, established the first economically successful South American airline, Sociedad Colombo-Alemana de Transportes Aéreos (SCADTA). Unlike other airlines in South America and the United States that were generally subsidized, SCAD-TA carried its own weight because there was a real need for its service. Von Bauer's airline flew from Barranquilla, the Colombian seaport on the Caribbean, up the Magdalena River, 650 miles to the capital at Bogotá. Depending on the weather, the trip between the two cities took anywhere from a week to a month; by air the journey was only seven hours. By 1926, von Bauer had turned SCADTA into a highly efficient enterprise and he began laying plans to span the Caribbean, connecting Colombia and the United States.

Von Bauer's intentions did not go unnoticed, and the U.S. military attaché in Colombia began sending reports about SCADTA to Major Henry H. ("Hap") Arnold, then an intelligence officer stationed in Washington. Arnold learned that the trans-Caribbean route would occasionally take SCADTA's aircraft over the Panama Canal. Fearing catastrophic consequences if a German-owned airline flew over the canal and into Florida, Arnold set out immediately to stop von Bauer.

In the 1920s, the Post Office Department underwrote commercial aviation through mail subsidies and hence controlled the development of the airlines. Arnold met with Postmaster General Harry New and asked that the Post Office do something to block von Bauer's entry into the United States. New told Arnold that he was powerless to act unless a competing American airline gave him the justification to stop SCADTA.

Arnold did not take von Bauer lightly, so he and three friends, Major Carl Spaatz, Major Jack Joulet, and John Montgomery, a former naval officer, organized the skeleton of an American airline to stop German advances in South America. They appropriately called the airline "Pan American Airways." By the summer of 1926 the paperwork for the airline had progressed far enough so that Arnold prepared to resign his commission and dedicate all of his time to Pan Am. But this was not to be.

In early September two events forced Arnold to reconsider his resignation from the army. On September 1, the first trans-Pacific flight, with a crew of five navy fliers, was reported missing. Just two days later the dirigible, *Shenandoah,* broke apart over Caldwell, Ohio, killing fourteen. In response to these disasters, Billy Mitchell, deeply concerned with the future of military aviation, broke his long silence and spoke out.

A close friend of Arnold, Mitchell stripped the veneer off military aviation, saying that the recent disasters were not accidents but were caused by inadequate and faulty equipment and were ". . . the direct result of incompetency, criminal negligence and almost treasonable administration of the national defense by the War and Navy Departments." This statement won Billy Mitchell his day in court and court-martial proceedings were brought against him. Now, with Mitchell drummed out of the army air corps, military aviation hit its lowest point since the end of the war. Arnold, Spaatz, and Joulet felt they could not desert the army at this crucial moment, and left Pan American solely in the hands of John Montgomery.

Left with nothing more than a paper airline, Montgomery still commanded a stack of documents, invoices, letters, and cancelled checks that represented what could be the greatest airline in the world. Paper or not, this potential was not lost on President Gerardo Machado of Cuba, who in late 1926 awarded Pan American exclusive rights to transfer mail from Havana to Florida. Even without a single aircraft in Pan Am's hangar, the Cuban contract was a worthy beginning.

While Montgomery looked for financial backing to purchase equipment, a thousand miles to the north in New York Juan Trippe and three close friends from college invited six other friends and relatives to invest in their new investment firm, the Aviation Corporation of America. The ten men who agreed to become partners had remarkably similar backgrounds. Their affinity was not a coincidence; they traveled in the same circles and they were among the richest and most powerful men in America. All were either bankers or aviators or both, each had attended a northeastern college, all were Republicans and athletes. They were also international in their outlook but, more important, they all had a history of making major business decisions and of having influence in the right places. Each partner contributed $25,000 to the corporation, really a pittance because the accumulated wealth of the board ran into the millions. The list of the board of directors read like a contemporary *Who's Who*:

W. Averell Harriman, a 1913 graduate of Yale, was known as a pretty fair polo player and served with the Bank of Manhattan, Western Union, and Guaranty Trust. Harriman was also a member of Skull and Bones. Edward O. McDonnell, graduate of the U.S. Naval Academy, retired as lieutenant commander in 1918 to pursue investment banking. Grover Loening, 1908 graduate of Columbia, had been general manager for the Wright Company before he founded his own company in 1918, Loening Aeronautical Engineering. He was an avid tennis player and sailor. John Hay Whitney, a graduate of Yale, had several banking and business interests. He was also a member of the Knickerbocker Club and the New York Yacht Club. Sherman Fairchild was president of Fairchild Aviation Corporation, Fairchild Aerial Surveys, and Fairchild Aerial Camera. Seymour Knox, cousin of the five-and-dime millionaire Frank Woolworth, was a 1920 graduate of Yale and a vice-president of Marine Trust.

Trippe and his college friends were younger, a bit less well established than the others; but they still had impressive credentials. Cornelius Vanderbilt Whitney was a handsome, blue-eyed member of a wealthy Baltimore family. Along with Trippe he had founded the Yale Flying Club and had been associated with Guaranty Trust. (In 1929, his wife, Marie Norton, would marry Averell Harriman.) John Hambleton was also from a prosperous Baltimore family, a member of the Yale Flying Club, and an ace in the First World War. He too was involved in banking. William Vanderbilt served with Commercial National Bank and Aquidneck National Exchange Bank of Newport and, like John Hay Whitney, was a member of the Knickerbocker and New York Yacht clubs. Trippe, the head of the investment firm, had a similarly impressive background.

Descended from an English family that had originally settled in Maryland, Juan Trippe was born in Seabright, New Jersey, on June 27, 1899, to Lucy Terry and Charles White Trippe. His mother had expected a daughter and had planned to name the child Juanita, for a favorite aunt. After his birth she changed the name to Juan and already life had begun to favor him. Years later, while he was bargaining in South America for landing rights for Pan American many Latin officials believed that with dark brown eyes and a

Spanish first name, he also had Latin blood in his veins. Because it helped ease negotiations, he did not discourage this myth.

Dividing his early life between the family residence in New Jersey, a town house on East 73rd Street just off Fifth Avenue in Manhattan, and a summer house in East Hampton on Long Island, Trippe had two distinct sides to his nature. The cool, conservative, shy Trippe was a product of his father, who had mounted a modest fortune through his investment firm, Trippe, Schuyler and Company. The adventurous Trippe, the side that compelled him to go into aviation rather than the family business, came from an early ancestor, Lieutenant John Trippe, who had fought the Barbary pirates, thereby winning the Sword of Valor.

By 1916, now broad-shouldered and at his adult height of six feet, Trippe entered Yale. During his freshman year his almost debilitating shyness surfaced. At an initiation ceremony Trippe was required to give a speech but he was so terrified that his face puckered and he was unable to utter a single word—thereby gaining his collegiate and somewhat mocking nickname, "Mummy." He left Yale after his first year and joined the naval flying corps, qualifying as a bombing pilot. But he did not see action. At the end of the war he returned to Yale and helped form the Yale Flying Club. After graduation at twenty-three, he followed his father's lead and joined Lee Higginson and Company as a bond salesman.

Unlike the other members of the Aviation Corporation, Trippe's primary interest was aviation, not finance. He had left Wall Street in 1923 and with John Hambleton had bought nine surplus navy seaplanes to set up Long Island Airways. The limited service, flying vacationers to the New York shore and to Atlantic City, was never profitable. This—combined with a flawed organization in which Trippe served as president, sales manager, and occasionally as a pilot and chief mechanic—forced the airline to close after less than two years of operation.

Though 1925 was disastrous for Trippe it marked the beginning of a whole new era for commercial aviation. Until 1925 commercial aviation had to rely on the quirks of a wary flying public to support it and—as demonstrated by the collapse of Long Island Airways and dozens of other airlines during the era—flying passengers was not a profitable business. But through the enactment of the Kelly Mail Act in 1925, the financial structure of commercial aviation was radically altered. With guaranteed government subsidies from the Post Office Department, an airline could collect as much as three dollars a pound for the delivery of mail. No longer would airlines have to rely on occasional passengers to pay the bills.

The stampede was on. Like so many others, Trippe, Hambleton, Whitney, and Vanderbilt realized that the potential financial success that could be achieved through the Kelly Act was nearly boundless. Hoping to win the first government airmail contract, each invested $25,000, forming Eastern Air Transport. At the same time another group, led by John O'Ryan under the banner of Colonial Airways, amassed $200,000, also hoping to take the first mail contract.

Rather than enter into a bidding war, however, the two groups merged under Colonial's name, handily winning Civil Air Mail Route One, New York to Boston. But, while the line was economically expedient, cooperation between the two factions did not last. Trippe had visions of greater and grander things—he wanted to improve efficiency by buying new Fokker Trimotors and carrying passengers. O'Ryan, happy with things as they were, would not listen to Trippe. The bickering lasted for months. Rather than endure the financial caution of O'Ryan's majority, Trippe and his partners sold out and organized the Aviation Corporation of America. Through the

Pan Am's Alameda, California terminal building (Pan American World Airways)

Wah Sun Choy (San Francisco Chronicle)

The Hawaii Clipper en route to Honolulu (Pan American World Airways)

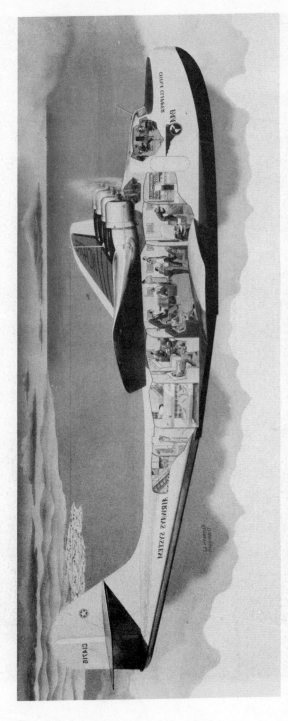

Profile of the Martin flying boat, from the bow: the bridge, the galley, crew's quarters (these two compartments were later reversed), lounge, two sitting rooms, toilets, and the aft stairs (Pan American World Airways)

The Martin flying boat on San Francisco Bay (Pan American World Airways)

One of the Martin Clipper's two private sitting rooms. The flying boats were heavily influenced by the art deco style. (Pan American World Airways)

Dinner and lunch were served in
grand style with linen, china, silver,
and heavy water goblets. The steward is Ivan Parker, who served
aboard the Hawaii Clipper in the
summer of 1938. (Pan American
World Airways)

The berths were only used on the
long night flights between California
and Hawaii. On succeeding nights,
the passengers stayed in hotels on
the islands. (Pan American World
Airways)

Juan Trippe as a Navy aviator in 1918 (Pan American World Airways)

Juan Trippe with Charles Lindbergh, Pan Am's technical advisor. Lindbergh made numerous test flights in the Martin Clippers. (Pan American World Airways)

The China Clipper at the Pearl Harbor landing dock (Library of Congress)

The walk from the landing dock to the Pearl Harbor terminal was a beautiful introduction to Hawaii (Pan American World Airways)

Glenn L. Martin, Martin Marietta Corporation

The Pan Am Hotel at Midway. The lounge and dining room were in the center and each wing had about twenty rooms. (Pan American World Airways)

first half of 1927 the corporation wallowed about trying
desperately to invest in some transportation system, at one
point even bidding on a dog-team route in Alaska but failing to
win even that.

Meanwhile in Florida, Pan American, still without a
single aircraft, floundered near bankruptcy. John Montgomery had one competitor, Florida Airways, which was well
organized and financed. Backed by a group led by Richard
Hoyt, Wall Street's aviation kingmaker from the investment
firm of Hayden and Stone, the airline was moderately successful until two of its three aircraft crashed. Even with solid
money behind it, without a mail contract and with only one
airplane, Florida Airways was just about worthless.

Though Pan Am had neither real financial backing nor
any aircraft it had managed to survive, and since it was the
only American international airline, paper or not, its mail
contract made it look more and more like a solid investment.
Then in the spring the Post Office Department surprised
nearly everyone when it granted Pan Am exclusive rights to
transport mail to Cuba. With mail contracts for both direc-
tions across the Straits of Florida, Montgomery found himself
in a powerful and potentially highly profitable position.

None of this was lost on Trippe or Richard Hoyt.
Through the summer the two jockeyed with one another,
trying to purchase a controlling interest in Pan American. But
each deal fell through. Finally, on October 3, just sixteen days
before the mail contracts were required to begin, Trippe,
Hoyt, and Montgomery settled on a new financial arrangement. They agreed to form a new holding company, The
Aviation Corporation of the Americas, in which each party
would buy a one-third interest and Pan American Airways
would become the corporation's operating company. The
power and financing really resided in Trippe and Hoyt,
though, for Montgomery could not line up adequate banking

and only purchased 20 percent of the new corporate stock. The remaining 80 percent was divided equally between Trippe's and Hoyt's backers. The total investment in Pan American amounted to $500,000, a woefully small sum to finance an international airline, even in 1927, but the money had come from the most powerful aeronautical and financial interests of the time, who represented an aggregate wealth of nearly one billion dollars.

Though the financial underpinnings of Pan American were solid enough, the marriage of the three groups was never really very satisfactory. In a short time Montgomery was forced out of the corporation. The separation proved bitter and Montgomery would try some years later to form another airline to compete with Trippe, but would fail. Hoyt and Trippe did not get along much better. Hoyt did not trust Trippe, then barely twenty-eight, to head the corporation, so he demanded that he be appointed chairman of the board and that Trippe be relegated to the inferior position of president of the corporation's subsidiary, Pan American Airways. Although this was a move of immediate utility, as time passed Hoyt's power diminished, since the day-to-day control over Pan American eventually became the dominant factor in controlling the corporation.

From the beginning Trippe proved that he was in charge. With just weeks to piece together the airline before the Cuban and U.S. mail-contract options expired, Trippe hired three men who would stay with Pan American until their last days. Each in his own way would do the daily hard labor that turned Montgomery's pile of paper into the world's foremost airline. André Priester, a frail, balding Dutchman who had previously worked for Royal Dutch Airlines, would become the line's chief engineer. Edwin Musick, a savvy, technically expert pilot, would become Pan Am's chief pilot and train Trippe's cadre of transoceanic pilots. Charles Lindbergh, fresh from his trans-Atlantic solo, would serve as Pan American's technical advisor.

Just over two weeks later, on October 19, Cy Caldwell made the one-hour-and-ten-minute mail flight to Havana—in a Fairchild floatplane borrowed from West Indian Aerial Express—marking America's entry into international commercial aviation.

Pan American was in business and, as Hap Arnold hoped, von Bauer was stopped.

5

Honolulu

July 24, 1938

*A*T TWO HUNDRED MILES OUT OF HONOLULU the first soft pink light of dawn spread over the Hawaii Clipper. Ahead of the flying boat the far western sky, stained cobalt by the lingering traces of night, looked like a vast painted backdrop.

During the night Parker had turned down the cabin heat, and as the passengers filtered into the lounge there was still a slight chill in the air. As Parker poured coffee for each of the men he told them that they could expect to land in an hour and a half.

Sitting behind First Officer Mark Walker, Radio Officer McCarty was taking the 6:00 A.M. weather reports from Makapuu Point on Oahu. The message was short. Reaching across the bridge McCarty handed it to Terletsky: "Light breeze at Pearl, temperature 75, light showers at 3000 feet off

Diamond Head." By this time the morning light had washed away the night and as Terletsky looked up from the message he spotted a dark mound on the horizon. He asked McCarty to go below and have Third Officer Sauceda pass the weather report along to the passengers telling them that he had sighted Molokai and they would see Mauna Kea on the left side shortly.

Near 7:00 Terletsky intersected Maui and set a north-west course for the short run to Honolulu. The cool air of 10,000 feet warmed as they approached Oahu, and at 3,000 feet the full force of the tropical air invaded the cabin. West of Diamond Head, as predicted, a rainbow spilled from a rain cloud. On the final approach over Pearl Harbor Terletsky signaled for full power. Once again the roar of the engines blasted through the ship. Banking and then drifting to the left, the Clipper dropped lower until finally the muffled rush of water told Terletsky that they had touched down.

The world was suddenly different. For nearly eighteen hours they had been held in a secure, free-floating envelope, but now the world seemed oppressive. The freedom of flight was gone as the ship lumbered toward the dock, heaving with the swells. Choy looked toward the shore. A light breeze ruffled the harbor and ahead heavily fronded palms partially obscured the Pan American terminal. At the dock the ground crew scurried about lashing the Clipper with bow and stern lines. The engines chugged, then stopped. Though there were sounds outside from the ground crew, without the engine background noise, it seemed silent. French, stretching to his full height, touched the gray ceiling with his hands. "We made it! Some flying machine, eh, Watson?" Choy nodded in agreement.

Reversing the process of eighteen hours ago, the passengers stepped up the metal stairs and then down onto the dock where each was greeted with a white ginger lei. Huntington and Dr. Reichert rushed off for the hospital while the others were directed through the terminal and then outside to the automobile that would take them to the Royal Hawaiian in Waikiki.

The crew remained in the Clipper; it would take half an hour to secure the ship. Then they would drive into downtown Honolulu and spend the night at the Alexander Young Hotel. While Parker cleaned the passenger quarters, the flight crew shut down the Clipper and Terletsky scribbled in the log. Terletsky wrote nothing to mark this flight as any different from the previous 228 flights to the Far East; after three years, the procedures were routine, everything worked very smoothly. But from this day on, Flight 229 would be singularly different.

While Choy unpacked his suitcase in his room at the Royal Hawaiian, two Japanese naval officers on Saipan, 3,800 miles across the Pacific, were making last-minute preparations for their 115-mile trip to Guam.

Perhaps for as long as three years, shortly after the Clippers began making regular flights to Guam, Japanese agents had occasionally slipped onto Guam on several occasions to observe the landings and departures of the Clippers and check on the activities at the small naval base at Sumay. This operation had been well planned and had gone almost entirely unnoticed by Americans on Guam. Now the espionage ring would be put to its hardest test so far. Acting on information that Wah Sun Choy was on the Hawaii Clipper, two Japanese officers planned to sail to the eastern shore of Guam and rendezvous with the Hawaii Clipper on July 29.

This Japanese espionage ring was not a complete secret. On August 21, a few weeks after the Hawaii Clipper landed in Pearl Harbor, the Federal Bureau of Investigation in Portland, Oregon, filed a report based on these Japanese activities on Guam. A letter enclosed with the report explained what the informant, a former U.S. Marine, had seen:

I am going to give you some information you may or may not already know. I can prove my statement by a witness that was with me. He, however, is in Virginia, but you can reach him through your official channels. This information was quieted down by certain people at the time and I will mention no names in this letter, but if you are interested you can have one of your men call on me, and providing they are asked in the right spirit, I will answer any of the questions you might care to know, that might help clear up the crash at sea of the Pan American Clipper.

You people suspect foul play, and I have looked for it for the past two years.

There is a powerful Japanese spy ring working in Guam, right under the nose of the Island Government. I lived on the island for three years. I was at Sumay attached to the U.S. Marine Corps. I did refrig. work for Pan American and can prove all this by letters of recommendation, and my discharge from the U.S. Marine Corps. Also you can check it there in Wash, D.C.

I spent many days of my three yrs. there exploring the island, and actually caught the Japs working about a 24 inch signal light, there is a lot more to the story and many facts you should know. But too much to write, and I might say the wrong thing, and I don't want to get in trouble. This information is given in good will, and you might find the answer to many of the 'leaks' of government affairs if you check.

I haven't told this to anyone else, as you know the

trouble you can get into. But I can tell you some
things that will make *several* people sorry in the end.

It's a damn shame they get away with it, but it
does. They have a spy ring, with the head of it right in
the center of town. I've seen it in action and almost got
my fingers burnt, but I can tell you now without any
hindrance.

They land 40ft. motor dories off of Jap schooners
and destroyers right on the island . . . . ''

When the FBI met with the former marine he explained
what he had seen and pinpointed the location, on the eastern
shore of Guam where he and a policeman had seen the Japanese
land. The Portland FBI office filed this letter and a typed
four-page report of his oral statement in Washington, D.C., as
Crime on the High Seas. The agent concluded the report by
writing: "It is believed significant to note that this man appeared
very sincere and honest in his contentions during the interview
Agent had with him. He also appears to be intelligent and gives
the impression he knows what he is talking about."

Japanese officers at Saipan knew the procedures at the Pan
Am base intimately. Under the cover of night they would sail to
Guam and stay at a fisherman's cabin on the east coast until July
28. After dark they would make the fifteen-mile hike across the
island and meet the Hawaii Clipper at Sumay.

Choy stepped to the window of his room. Still early
morning, only 9:00, the Sunday crowd had not arrived on the
beach below. A dark-skinned man lugged a heavy surfboard to
the water's edge and a few scattered couples spread beach
blankets on the smooth white sand. Framing the quiet scene,
Diamond Head towered over the bathers. How idyllic it is,
Choy thought. Beauty such as this always made him feel
melancholy.

6

The Middle Kingdom Space Machine Family

December 1929-November 1933

As early as December 1929, during a European vacation, Trippe had concluded a secret preliminary agreement with G.E. Woods-Humphrey, director of Imperial Airways, to jointly inaugurate trans-Atlantic flights. In the following spring Trippe and Woods-Humphrey signed a formal contract creating a subsidiary, Pan American-Imperial Airways, in which each company owned half interest. But it was not a cooperative venture at all; instead, it was based on vigorous political competition and nationalism.

As the military's importance diminished after the war, aviation became the worldwide symbol of prestige, the hallmark of the modern industrial state, and the international airlines illustrated this better than any other phase of aviation. The Pan Am-Imperial agreement was made so that neither the United States nor Great Britain would suffer the interna-

tional disgrace of flying the Atlantic second. The Pan Am-
Imperial subsidiary was also a product of intricate political
considerations.

Unlike maritime law, which grants freedom of the seas,
aviation law does not account for a parallel concept. Landing
in or flying over a foreign country is not a right but a privilege
given in exchange for political considerations. This restriction
was perhaps the fundamental concept that determined how
international aviation developed around the world. So when
Pan American and Imperial agreed to share the Atlantic the
agreement was based on reciprocal landing rights; no other
country could invade the Pan Am-Imperial route. Tied to the
prestige and politics of aviation, a third element, technology,
was the decisive factor in determining who would fly and
control the world's trade routes.

As demonstrated by Europe's early link with Asia, flying
relatively long distances over land was not at all difficult even
in 1931. By making a series of short flights, stopping for fuel
and repairs, a journey of almost any duration could be made.
Trans-oceanic flights were an entirely different matter. Even
by hopping from island to island the best commercial aircraft
of the early 1930s could not span the oceans. The interisland
distances were too great, so in the end it was also technology,
not just politics, that determined who flew the oceans first.

Acutely aware of the political and technical problems that
lay ahead in the Atlantic, André Priester and Charles Lindbergh met regularly in the afternoons with Juan Trippe
through late 1930 and early 1931, trying to develop an orderly
plan for Pan American's expansion. Occasionally, these meet-
ings lasted into the night, and the three men retired to Trippe's
small Park Avenue apartment nearby, where the talks were
carried on through dinner.

Trippe really had only two choices for routes. One route
traced the Atlantic through Newfoundland and Iceland, termi-

nating in London. The second skipped across the north Pacific rim: from Alaska to Siberia, Japan, and south to Nanking, China. By hopping from base to base both of the routes would be within the capabilities of a new generation of flying boats. Trippe was certain that the technical problem of flying the oceans could be solved, so he decided where to fly based solely on economics. The north Pacific route to China, though reasonably short, was chancy. Priester was not sure if it could be flown during the harsh arctic winter on a regular basis; if not, the only alternative would be to make the Pacific crossing over mid-ocean, which was not financially attractive because of the vast distances between the islands. Hawaii, the first landfall west of San Francisco, is isolated from California by 2,500 miles of ocean. Manila lies another 5,500 miles to the west, while the remaining Asian capitals are thousands of miles beyond the Philippines. In the Atlantic, London, a major financial center, is only 3,400 miles from New York, and dozens more European cities lie just miles across the English channel. With the greatest concentration of wealth, population and industry located along the eastern seaboard of the United States, a line connecting New York and London was Trippe's first choice.

In 1931, when Trippe finally asked for bids for the new trans-oceanic flying boats, the order really amounted to the absurd. Nothing like them had ever been built and Trippe's requirements for speed, range, and load-carrying ability went far beyond the wildest dreams of most aeronautical engineers. Most aircraft manufacturers in the United States declined even to bid on the flying boats, save two—Glenn Martin and Igor Sikorsky.

Obsessed with building airplanes, Glenn Martin accepted Trippe's offer even though he knew it was a potentially disastrous business decision. In 1931 Martin was near bankruptcy and his business associates warned him that there would be no profit and a lot of grief in building the giant boats for Pan American. Lassiter Milburn, Martin's chief engineer, and C.A. Van Dusen, the company's business manager, demanded that Martin refuse the project, arguing that it was much too complicated and might put him out of business. Martin turned all of this away with a wave of his hand. He was intrigued by Trippe's proposal. He wanted to be the one manufacturer who could make a vision real. Even though Martin lacked Trippe's business sense, he was not entirely unlike Trippe.

He was skillful, rational and a talented aircraft manufacturer. He once told a reporter: "The way to build aircraft or do anything else worthwhile is to think out quietly every detail, analyze every situation that may possibly occur and then never stop until you have produced the thing you started to make." Trippe might well have uttered the same words.

Martin was also incautious, enough to be very successful. Like many of his generation, he started in aviation as a barnstormer, but unlike the others he made enough money—stunting at county fairs in California—to start his own aircraft manufacturing company. Though he wore an outlandish all-black flying outfit that earned him the nickname "The Flying Dude," and won many firsts in barnstorming, one competing barnstormer described him as being about as joyful as an undertaker. Martin was a builder and a worker, not a dude. Early in his life he dedicated himself to the pursuit of excellence to the exclusion of everything else. He relaxed by hunting and fishing and pursued his pleasures with the same single-minded determination he followed in his work. So preoccupied was he with tracking his prey, one wondered if he enjoyed sport at all. He never married; throughout his life his only close female relationship was with his mother, who really served as his business partner.

In 1928, firmly established as a quality aeronautical

manufacturer, Martin bought 1,200 acres just outside Baltimore in Middle River, Maryland for a new factory. Here the trans-Pacific Clippers would be built. Martin submitted a bid of $2 million to Trippe for three flying boats. Trippe promptly rejected the offer, countering with $1 million. Trippe and Martin haggled through eight different contracts until they *finally* settled on a final price of $417,000 for each boat. The price really amounted to a giveaway; when Van Dusen heard the boats were going for less than $650,000, he howled, telling Martin that they would lose between $700,000 and $900,000. As it turned out, Martin did lose heavily on the three flying boats, and if it had not been for an unexpected contract from the Army to produce a bomber, building the seaplanes would have ruined Martin.

Even though Martin lost money on the Clippers, they cost Trippe a fortune. The popular DC–2, which was used by most domestic carriers in the early 1930s, cost a mere $80,000 per airplane, and another smaller Clipper to be built by Sikorsky, which Trippe ordered along with the Martins, cost less than half Martin's bid of $210,000 each. But Martin's Clipper would be worth every penny; the boat would be a dream made real, the queen of the skies.

But from the beginning Imperial could not match Trippe's plans. In the later half of 1931, the British realized that they could not develop a trans-oceanic transport until much later in the decade. Realizing that if Great Britain did not build a trans-oceanic aircraft she would cancel the Pan Am-Imperial cooperation agreement, Trippe thought once more about the great-circle route to China.

In order to defend Pan American from a potential blockade of the Atlantic by the British, Trippe in midsummer dispatched Charles and Anne Morrow Lindbergh to survey the route to China. Following the route mapped out the previous spring, the Lindberghs flew their Lockheed Sirius

across the fogbound straits of the Bering Sea down the coast of
Asia to Nanking. Technically and politically the flight went as
well as could be expected. Even the Russians were exception-
ally cooperative. But precisely because of the Soviet interest,
this route would not be flown in the 1930s. In one of the very
few intrusions into Pan American's affairs, the State Department, fearing communist demands for reciprocal landing
rights in the United States, told Trippe that he could not land
in Soviet territory. Blocked in the north Pacific, Trippe's
choices were considerably narrowed.

With the Pan Am-Imperial agreement disintegrating,
Trippe set out to organize a line to Europe that would not
require British cooperation. Newfoundland, Iceland, and
Denmark were receptive to the idea. Still, the route was
fraught with political complications, covering both sides of the
world. Trippe continued talks in Europe while he opened
negotiations with the Chinese.

Established in 1929 by the Curtiss-Wright Corporation,
the China National Aviation Corporation—literally translated, the Middle Kingdom Space Machine Family—flew
between Hangchow and Shanghai. But it had been a dismal
failure. Curtiss-Wright refused to underwrite CNAC's losses
and pulled out, leaving it solely in the hands of the Chinese
government. Trippe, on the other hand, knew that both the
trans-Pacific line and CNAC could be profitable, but only if
they worked in concert. On March 31, 1933, Trippe nailed
down a good chunk of the Pacific line when he signed a
contract with the Nationalist government and bought a 45
percent share of CNAC.

While the Pan Am-Imperial contract was based on competition, the Pan Am-CNAC agreement was founded on mu-
tual need. It was also a product of the eccentricities of Pacific
politics. China needed modern, efficient transportation but

could not supply it on its own. In 1933, land transportation in China was primitive by any measure. It took weeks to travel between cities; coastal pirates roamed the East China Sea, making steamer travel not only slow but dangerous. With a land transportation system that barely worked, and with the growing specter of a Japanese invasion, the technology Trippe offered was naturally very attractive to China. At the same time, because of the Japanese threat, Chiang Kai-shek would not allow Pan American to operate within China's borders under its own name. If China had granted Pan Am, or any other airline, operating rights within its borders, Japan would have demanded similar privileges. So to circumvent a Japanese commercial invasion, which would have been followed by greater Japanese control over China, the Chinese government maintained majority control over CNAC. Forced to operate in China as Pacific America, Pan American did not have actual landing rights in China, only operational control over CNAC. This meant that the trans-Pacific Clippers could never land within China. Still this was all the entree Trippe needed.

But there was another, more subtle advantage for Trippe in this agreement. Besides gaining exclusive and monopolistic control of China's skies, Trippe, as a minority partner, could not be forced by other airlines to trade off valuable landing rights in China. As long as Japan remained a threat, Trippe's control of Chinese commercial aviation, at the exclusion of all other countries, was assured. Trippe and Chiang Kai-shek had the best of both worlds—Chiang got a modern airline while keeping the Japanese out of China and Trippe secured operational control of a government-guaranteed monopoly which he would later link with his trans-Pacific Clippers.

About the same time Trippe opened negotiations with the Chinese, an undercurrent of paranoia was sweeping through some segments of the navy: war with Japan was already seen as a real possibility. Since the early 1920s, virtually every quarter of the American military suspected Japan of fortifying the Mandates but the concern did not match reality. Until Japan's withdrawal from the League of Nations in 1933, the Imperial Navy adhered to the letter of the nonfortification treaties. It was not until after 1933 that the Japanese build-up in Micronesia began. Still, hard evidence of Japan's expansion in the islands was not a prerequisite for these concerns. When the Joint Board weighed Japan's potential strength in Micronesia against America's waning Pacific naval power, they knew that the United States would lose the Philippines and Guam within the first weeks of a war with Japan. In April 1932 the Office of Naval Intelligence no longer speculated on the possibility of war with Japan but now in a confidential report numbered 104, titled *Political Forces: Japanese-American Relations*, openly predicted war:

> . . . Relations between Japan and the United States have daily become more strained. . . . This critical situation does not date from the present but has a background extending over many years. The cross points of the two nations are China and the islands in the Southern Pacific (Philippines and Guam).
>
> To judge from purely political and economic viewpoints one might say that war could occur at any time, but the reason that there has as yet been no open conflict between the two nations is due to the military and financial conditions existing in both countries. . . .
>
> The defense plan of the United States is prepared with Japan as the essential enemy, while in turn the Japanese Navy is so planned as to have the United States for its objective."

The Washington Naval Treaty had sealed the fate of the

western Pacific and in 1932 Naval Intelligence wrote off the Philippines as a lost cause:

> . . . Manila Bay is well laid out in the front, the entrance, but the sides are as doors opened. If the Japanese sent in two divisions of troops with the help of some naval vessels they could capture the place within three weeks time. So the United States may not be able to defend the Philippine Islands when the American-Japanese conflict is started.
> . . . Therefore, the Philippine Islands are not expected to be very useful to the United States in her fight with Japan. That is why Japan dares to do as she pleases without fear of the United States.

It all must have seemed hopeless. By 1932, the Japanese army had already invaded and conquered Manchuria, while the Imperial navy looked longingly at the rich oil fields in the Dutch East Indies and prepared to move deeper into Micronesia. The American navy, on the other hand, had been stymied by the Washington Treaty, Congressional action, and by a growing popular policy of isolationism. In the past fifteen years the navy had accomplished nothing more than establishing over and over again the strategic value of Hawaii, Midway, Wake, and Guam for the defense of the Pacific in the coming war. For another two years the American navy hopelessly thrashed about looking for some way to fortify these islands. Not until the spring of 1934 did the navy finally find the ruse it needed when Pan American began to lay the foundations for the Pacific bases the navy itself could not build.

Under the terms of the CNAC contract, Pan Am was required to institute mail delivery no later than July 7, 1933, or suffer the loss of its option to fly the lucrative coastal line. On the 7th the Chinese minister of communications refused to turn over the first mail shipment. He did so because he was attempting to play Pan American off against Lufthansa's Asian subsidiary, Eurasia Airlines, which was willing to pay virtually any price for the exclusive right to fly the China coast. This delay was serious, so serious that the American consulate in Shanghai forwarded a confidential report to the Division of Far Eastern Affairs at the State Department in Washington:

> . . . . If this plan, so important to the United States, is
> to be carried out, it is vitally important that the sector
> between Shanghai and Canton be operated by
> American interests under some arrangement or other.
> If rights to the operation between Shanghai and
> Canton are accorded to the German interests, it is hard
> to see how plans of Pan American Airways for a
> through American air transport service to the Far East
> can ever materialize.

The future of American aviation in the Pacific directly hinged on Pan American outmaneuvering Lufthansa. On July 7, Pan American personnel managed to find enough mail on their own to technically meet the terms of the contract but the first CNAC mail flight did not resolve the underlying financial problems. Through July and into August Pan Am continued to offer the original agreement of 10 percent while the Chinese maintained their new demand for 30 percent. Finally in late summer Pan Am set out to bluff the Chinese into accepting 10 percent by organizing a mock air route between Manila and Hong Kong, which would not include the main cities of China.

It was a bluff of extravagant proportions—Pan American

did not have rights into either Hong Kong or Manila, and such a limited route could never have been profitable. But the bluff worked. The enthusiasm in both Hong Kong and Manila for the service was so overwhelming that the business community in Shanghai feared that if Pan Am opened the Hong Kong-Manila line they would lose their central position in China. Since Eurasia was still years away from actually developing routes and bringing aircraft to Asia, China was left with little choice. China paid Pan Am's 10 percent. On October 23, 1933, CNAC began regular air service along the China coast.

While in the later stages of negotiation with China, Juan Trippe was also trying to secure a Far Eastern terminus in China for future trans-Pacific flights from Imperial Airways. Only Macao and Hong Kong could serve Trippe's needs since they were the only neutral points outside China itself. Trippe believed that Macao, small and underdeveloped, could not attract American businessmen 8,000 miles across the Pacific but that the glamor, excitement and business of Hong Kong could. When Trippe wrote to Woods-Humphrey for his help in obtaining rights into Hong Kong, predictably he found himself in a tough bargaining situation. In return for his words of aid to the government Woods-Humphrey wanted Trippe to give Imperial participation in CNAC's coastal line. Woods-Humphrey also offered long term rights through Newfoundland:

> Although I have no authority for saying so, I cannot help feeling that if we secure this permission you would be very much more likely to get the full term authorisation to operate via Newfoundland instead of the eight years mentioned in a recent telegram.

This offer must have been very attractive to Trippe. It

was all that he needed to span the oceans—rights into Hong Kong would have guaranteed the success of the trans-Pacific route and long-term authorization through Newfoundland would have done the same for the Atlantic line. But Trippe had other options. Macao was a viable alternative to Hong Kong and for the time being, Trippe, on his own, had secured rights through Newfoundland. All Trippe needed from Imperial was landing rights at Hong Kong, though, so on October 3 Trippe replied to Woods-Humphrey, explaining his relationship with CNAC:

> As to the sector between Canton and Shanghai, I believe it is definitely established that the Chinese government will not permit foreign companies to operate along this coast in their own name. It is only through our very substantial participation in the national air lines that the program has been developed. . . .

Negotiations with Wood-Humphrey typified Trippe's freedom to conclude agreements that could affect foreign policy. Except in the case of landing rights in Siberia, the State Department allowed Trippe to do pretty much as he pleased; if that meant dealing with presidents, dictators, or corporate officials, fine.

With near absolute authority, Trippe decreed when and where Pan American spread its wings. Where Juan Trippe succeeded, Pan Am prospered. Trippe accomplished all this through the most basic business tactics: he knew how to use power, he knew how to make a deal—whether it was in Cuba, China, the State Department, or the White House—and he knew how to make the deal stick.

To a casual observer who might have seen Trippe walking down 42nd Street, his large frame, round face, and clumsy manner did not make him appear to be the hard-driving executive he was. This had always been so. While attending Yale he had been characterized as a "big, phlegmatic, collegiate bear" and it was said that if a poll had been taken based on appearance, Trippe may well have been voted the least likely to succeed. This was not altogether a disadvantage, though. Other airline executives and government officials with whom he had to deal were often caught off guard by his quiet, almost self-effacing manner; as a result, Trippe usually got exactly what he wanted.

Because of the freedom allotted him, Trippe directed the early course of American international aviation—deciding what routes Pan Am flew in Latin America, fixing Pan American's course across the Atlantic and Pacific, and determining when and how much he would trade for landing rights in Hong Kong. This freedom had not been given blindly, for it also served the government quite well. Trippe's negotiations with foreign governments created informal relationships that could be recognized or dismissed by the State Department. This symbiotic relationship had been especially fruitful to both sides during Pan Am's formative years in Latin America. But when Trippe moved into China, the political scene, fraught with explosive possibilities, was much too complex to be left entirely under Pan Am's command.

In spite of Trippe's elaborate planning in China, his primary attention remained focused on the Atlantic. By the summer of 1933, the Pan American-Imperial contract had collapsed, but by this time also, Trippe had a good shot at securing one of two Atlantic routes. Some years earlier Marcel Bouilloux-Lafont, director of Aeropostale, Air France, had suggested that Pan Am and Air France share the exclusive concession he had won from the Portuguese, flying a south Atlantic route through the Azores and Lisbon. This was an extremely attractive offer, the weather was good, and the route was a way to avoid butting up against British power. The alternative line, across the north Atlantic, skipped from New York to Newfoundland, Iceland, and the Faeroe Islands to Denmark.

On July 9, 1933, sure that Pan American would fly the Atlantic, Trippe sent Charles and Anne Lindbergh on a survey of the northern route. Flying in the same red-and-black Lockheed Sirius they used on the great-circle route to China, the Lindberghs meticulously surveyed the area around Greenland, criss-crossed Iceland and England. But late in the summer, as they flew over the French coast, word came: the Atlantic negotiations had failed.

Through the early 1930s, Newfoundland suffered more than most countries from the Depression. On occasion, citizen anger erupted into street violence. Through 1933, the island verged on anarchy as mobs stormed the Newfoundland Executive Council demanding government action to solve the economic crisis. With the situation nearly out of control, Great Britain stepped in and revoked the island's dominion status.

Acting with broad strokes, one of Britain's first actions was to cancel Pan American's landing rights. Without the first and most crucial refueling base, the north Atlantic crossing was impossible. Trippe turned to the French for help, but it was too late. Through nonperformance, Air France had lost its concession, and when Trippe approached Portugal on his own, he was denied landing rights in the Azores. It was not really Lisbon that blocked Trippe. Resolved that Imperial and Pan Am would inaugurate trans-Atlantic service simultaneously or not at all, Britain pressured the Portuguese to deny Trippe's reapplication for landing rights.

Trippe did not take any of this lightly. A few years later, when Imperial clamored for help in finding island bases in the Pacific, Trippe did little to help Imperial.

7

The Alliance

May 1934-January 1935

PRIOR TO 1934, the navy officially had very little contact with Pan Am, but later this relationship became so entwined that it was difficult to determine where the needs of one left off and the other's began. The issue that formed this relationship was one of signal importance—the Pacific air bases.

In 1934, Pan American had just moved from the Chanin Building into new offices diagonally across 42nd Street, occupying two floors of the Chrysler Building. On a balmy May day Pan Am's board of directors gathered on the 59th floor for its first annual meeting in the new offices. There was some excitement about this meeting, more than in past years. The company had been doing very well. Profits were up in spite of the Depression, the Martin Clippers were nearing completion, but most important, Juan Trippe was going to give his report outlining their progress in the Atlantic. After taking their seats, the board turned to Trippe, who was standing at the head of the table.

Without introduction Trippe looked down the table and bluntly began, "Gentlemen, we are about to fly the Pacific."

It was a typical Trippe tactic. Many of his most important decisions were made just this way, without the advice of the board. In fact, Trippe's decision to buy the Martin Clippers had been made secretly and it was not until months later that he informed the board of the purchase. That decision did not settle well and today's surprise announcement was equally resented. For a moment the board sat quietly; then the silence turned to rage. Why the Pacific? What happened to the Atlantic plans?

Methodically, Trippe explained how the British had blocked them at every crossing. Furthermore, he told them, with several million dollars of ocean-spanning equipment on order, they had to fly somewhere. Certainly British pressure had forced Trippe to abandon the Atlantic but there was also a compelling reason why Trippe had turned to the Pacific: bases were available without political complications. The United States owned scores of Pacific islands that Trippe knew could be used as stepping stones, refueling bases, for the long line to China. With these islands readily available, Trippe would not have to bargain with other countries for landing rights—the route from San Francisco to the shores of China could be completely American-controlled. But perhaps, too, Trippe had an inkling that the navy would help smooth the way for Pan Am.

The impact of Trippe's decision resounded all the way to Washington. Within days of the May meeting, the navy was already busy calculating what a commercial air route across to China would mean to Pacific strategy. The answer was obvious. It meant air bases of potential military value. It meant that at long last the process of fortifying the Pacific would begin.

On June 18, Commander J. F. Gillon of the Navy's Hydrographic Office, trying to determine who had responsibility for administering Wake Island, telephoned the State Department's historical adviser, Samuel Boggs: "Nothing has officially come before the navy but it appears that an American aviation firm is now considering establishing an air route which might touch Wake and lead to the Philippines." Sensing the first opportunity to expand its Pacific fortifications in over a decade, the navy acted quickly—but with notable caution because Gillon's question went far beyond the issue of jurisdiction; it was really a cloaked inquiry to determine which federal department would control the development of Pan Am's air bases. Pan American's decision to fly the Pacific was the navy's first opportunity to change the status of the Pacific atolls since the enactment of the Washington Treaty.

On June 20, Samuel Boggs returned Gillon's call and told him that neither he, the Treaty Division, nor the Legal Adviser's Office had any information to indicate that any branch of the executive department had jurisdiction over Wake. This apparently pleased Gillon; before hanging up, he said, "If the matter of the proposed air route definitely comes before the Navy Department, we presume that it would be a question for joint consideration by the Navy Department and the Department of State."

Trippe did not formally apply for rights across the mid-Pacific until October 3, but then he wrote a forceful three-page letter to the Secretary of the Navy Claude Swanson about Pan American's plans. Explaining that Pan Am planned to fly through Hawaii, Midway, Wake, Guam, and the Philippines en route to China, Trippe enticed Swanson by reminding him that the airline would build new settlements on Midway and Wake, both desert islands, in addition to servicing and communication facilities on all of the other islands. As though this were not enough, Trippe, in a thinly veiled reference to war preparations, offered to return control of the bases to the navy if it became necessary.

The navy responded instantly and positively. Just two days after the receipt of Trippe's letter, Acting Chief of Naval Operations, J. K. Taussig, endorsed the plan. His decision was based on sound research into Pan American's ability to build and maintain the long 8,000 mile air route. The navy's Bureau of Aeronautics, just completing a study of Pan American, concluded that Pan Am was better prepared than even the navy's aeronautical programs:

> . . . The operating personnel work harder and are further advanced in aerial navigation than the Navy. That, in percentage, the Pan American Airways have more planes for air navigation research, blind flying, and experimental work than the Navy. That the operating personnel are making every effort to prepare themselves for trans-oceanic work. That the Pan American airway's radio division has excellent radio equipment especially for taking radio bearings on high frequency sets. That the Pan American Airways have an excellent weather bureau.

Within days of Trippe's letter to Swanson, the White House and the navy acted simultaneously to expand America's control of the Pacific, beyond Pan Am's venture, to include the long neglected southern guano atolls. The islands Trippe needed for bases en route to China—Hawaii, Midway, Wake and Guam—were solidly under American control. There was no question about the sovereignty of these islands but the status of three strategic South Pacific atolls—Baker, Jarvis, and Howland—were of some concern because they were also claimed by Great Britain.

On October 16, Roosevelt sent a confidential memorandum to Secretary of State Cordell Hull in reference to the scores of islands that might be used by American aviation:

> Would you please familiarize yourself with the situation relating to these islands and then speak to me in regard to possible negotiation with Great Britain? The development of commercial aviation, as well as Naval operations, makes this whole subject of immediate importance.

Seeing that British commercial aviation could become a spoiler by diluting American control over the South Pacific atolls and thus indirectly opening more opportunities for Japan in the western Pacific, Roosevelt wanted as much of the Pacific as possible under U.S. jurisdiction. For the time being, British claims represented a far greater challenge to the expansion of American aviation than did the Japanese. Many of the islands in the Phoenix group, claimed by American whalers and guano miners in the nineteenth century, were solidly under American sovereignty, but the status of others was under dispute. Roosevelt wanted to solidify all disputed claims in favor of the United States now. The South Pacific islands of Baker, Howland, and Jarvis, listed as strategic by the navy, were claimed by both the United States and Great Britain. Marcus Island, northwest of Wake, also listed as strategic, was claimed by Japan and the United States. On the same day Roosevelt scribbled the memorandum to Cordell Hull, the navy, sensing the time was right to increase its power in the Pacific, also wrote to the State Department:

> The Navy Department desires to be informed whether there may be any diplomatic objection to the proposed transfer of Wake Island to the control and jurisdiction of the Navy Department for the purposes mentioned;

also what, if any, further negotiations or other actions
are contemplated to definitely settle the sovereignty of
Howland, Baker, Jarvis and Marcus Islands, and
what is the likelihood of their being made available for
the purpose above outlined. . . .

Essentially, the navy asked for control and subsequent
development of atolls that had been specifically delineated by
the 1922 naval treaty as areas of the Pacific that could not be
fortified. Though technically the atolls could be developed by
civilian interests, it is clear from the tone of the navy's October
16 letter that it saw the trans-Pacific line as largely a military
project. These were serious, far-reaching questions and the
State Department did not rush with a response. For nearly
two months after the receipt of the navy's letter the question
was batted about the State Department. On November 8, the
legal adviser, Ralph Hill, passed his opinion to Secretary
Hull's office. On the 28th the Division of Far Eastern Affairs
submitted its view of the problem to Hull and finally on
December 13, Acting Secretary of State William Phillips
wrote the distilled conclusions of the previous seven weeks and
forwarded them to Secretary Swanson:

> . . . I am of the opinion that were Wake Island placed
> under the control and jurisdiction of the Navy
> Department there would very likely result some
> adverse comment in Japan, and that such adverse
> comment would probably be avoided were Wake
> Island placed under the control and jurisdiction of one
> of the civilian departments of the Government, for
> instance, the Interior Department. However, should
> the Navy consider that from the point of view of the
> defense requirements of this country it would be highly
> desirable to place the public lands on Wake Island

under the jurisdiction of the Navy Department rather
than the jurisdiction of one of the civilian departments,
I do not believe that possible adverse reaction in Japan
should preclude such an action on the part of this
Government. . . .

This opinion was reached with considerable debate; certainly everyone realized the potential reaction from Japan. Still, State conceded that if navy control of Wake were considered important to the defense of the United States then the transfer should be made. Notably, one point that had been made by Ralph Hill back on November 8 was not included in Phillips's letter to Swanson. Concerned that the transfer of Wake to the navy might be a violation of the Washington Treaty, Hill wrote:

It would seem that we are precluded from establishing
a naval base or fortifications on Wake Island under
Article XIX of the treaty on the Limitation of Naval
Armament between the United States, the British
Empire, France, Italy and Japan . . .
In view of the foregoing provision a query might arise
as to whether a misconception might result from
placing Wake under the jurisdiction of the Navy
Department.

There could be no misconception; Phillips's letter to the navy stated openly that if the navy needed Wake for the defense of the United States then other considerations could be overlooked.

The navy's kinship with Pan Am was underscored by S. C. Hooper of the Navy Division of Communications, who saw Pan American acting as something of a commercial front for the navy. Writing to the Chief of Naval Operations in late

1934, Hooper explained that Pan American would be an invaluable ally in the Pacific:

> ... From the Navy's point of view, it is highly
> desirable to have adequate direction-finding service for
> airplanes established in the Pacific, and to train Navy
> personnel in the operation of such direction finders for
> both peace and wartime ...

At year's end the plan had fallen into place. Roosevelt signed an executive order placing Wake under the control of the navy and the navy in turn leased space at Pearl Harbor, Midway, Wake, and Guam to Pan American.

Flushed with this success the government saw that it had an interest in commercial aviation which far exceeded Pan American's immediate route across the mid-Pacific. Certainly, Roosevelt must have thought that if commercial aviation supplied a palatable ruse for bases in the mid-Pacific it could do the same in the South Pacific. Acting on this insight, shortly after the New Year, 1935, Roosevelt queried Secretary Swanson about the status of the American claim at Baker, Jarvis, and Howland islands. Since Roosevelt's last communication on this matter in October, nothing had been accomplished, but Swanson replied that the navy considered the islands strategically important.

Expansion in the Pacific was a thorny issue for the administration. The question of how to settle the claims without offending Japan or arousing the ire of Congress troubled Roosevelt and his cabinet for nearly three weeks. In a sort of round-table meeting officials from the State Department, Secretary Swanson, and Secretary of Commerce Daniel Roper debated this problem at length. They finally decided, and Roosevelt agreed, that the best way to assure the claim and block British and Japanese interests would be by landing

American colonists on the atolls. But this solved only part of the problem; how could they explain the purpose and expense of settling the three tiny and apparently meaningless atolls tucked far off in the South Pacific in the midst of the Depression? In fact, the answer was glaringly obvious. Commercial aviation supplied the ruse at Midway, Wake, and Guam. A civilian program, they reasoned, could do the same in the South Pacific.

From the conception of this idea until the return of the main exploratory force to Hawaii—nearly three months—this project was kept secret. But why would an innocent voyage—a civilian program—be classified secret? It was not an innocent expedition nor was it really a civilian operation. The government was searching for military outposts. As Billy Mitchell had pointed out nearly fifteen years earlier, the line from Honolulu to Manila was vulnerable to a flank attack by the Japanese through the length of Micronesia. So even though the Pan American line would greatly enhance the navy's position in the mid-Pacific, no one was sure that it could be kept open during wartime. Though longer and not as direct as the mid-Pacific route, the line through the Phoenix Islands, south of the equator, circumvented the Mandates. The navy reasoned this would be the safest route to the Far East and Australia in wartime.

Besides serving as a front for the military, commercial aviation also supplied the knowledge about the weather and helped develop equipment the military would need to conduct a war in the Pacific. A letter dated January 5, 1935, from the chief of naval operations to Secretary Swanson regarding the installation of radio equipment by Pan American quite directly explained the ultimate importance of commercial aviation to the military:

. . . As these facilities and services will be essential at

the outbreak of war, they should be established in the time of peace. This would insure the training of necessary personnel, the improvement of materiel and the reliability of these services for wartime use. . . .

The Commerce Department agreed to front the South Pacific cruise by supplying men and some equipment. The navy consented to partially finance the voyage and on January 23 Secretary Roper wrote to the War Department confirming the army's role in the project:

. . . In order to carry out the President's wishes in the matter, the cooperation of the Navy has been given. It may be necessary to ask certain cooperation from the War Department such as the possible loan of Army equipment at Honolulu, to be used in connection with the colonization. . . .

In early March, under the leadership of William Miller, the Commerce Department's superintendent of airways, the South Pacific expedition steamed out of Honolulu aboard the Coast Guard cutter *Itasca*. In the time since the decision had been made to make this voyage, Palmyra had been included in the islands Miller would visit, and on March 15 Miller typed up his first report from Palmyra. A frail atoll with little dry land, Palmyra lies one thousand miles directly south of Honolulu. Visiting Palmyra was perhaps a mistake. Miller concluded that other than serving as an emergency field or as a weather station the atoll would be of little use to aviation.

Again sailing south, Miller landed on Jarvis Island on March 26. Jarvis was larger and more substantial than Palmyra, but Miller decided that the island was unsuitable for use by seaplanes, although large enough to support ground facilities and a land runway. Miller named the first South

Pacific community after himself, Millersville, and left five
men and enough supplies for them to live comfortably until the
State Department decided that the American claim was secure.
The *Itasca* then sailed seven hundred miles west to Baker and
nearby Howland. While Miller considered Palmyra and Jarvis of dubious value, Howland and Baker appeared to be
exactly what military and commercial aviation needed. Both
were large and high enough to safely house complete aeronautical facilities. Lying on a direct line between Honolulu and
New Zealand/Australia, the islands were also ideally located
for refueling bases for flights to the south, and also for tactical
bases. Actually their use to the military was their primary
value. Unlike Guam, Howland and Baker were safely removed from the Mandates but still close enough to launch an
attack on Micronesia from the south.

As ordered, Miller conducted the expedition under tight
security. Only after the *Itasca* dropped anchor in Pearl Harbor did the Commerce Department reveal that Miller had
colonized the three atolls, and, as predicted, the story received
scant attention in the American press.

Miller had accomplished all that could be done for the
time being. In two years, when the defense posture shifted to
the south, time would reveal new possibilities. They would
point to Amelia Earhart, who, like Pan American, would
become an integral part of the Pacific defense strategy.

8

Midway

July 25, 1938

At 2:00 A.M. Midway time, while the rest of the base slept, the Midway base manager left his cozy room and went onto the windy sand dunes to take the day's weather readings for the Hawaii Clipper's run up to the atoll. After filling weather balloons with hydrogen, he then attached small candle-powered lanterns to them and sent them aloft. He noted the balloons' drift at thousand-foot intervals, and after they rose out of sight, he radioed this information and the surface conditions to Alameda.

With the Midway report and other observations from Pacific bases and ships, a weather chart for the Clipper route was made. Once this had been done Alameda radioed the information to Pearl Harbor in time for the base manager, John Boyle, to draw up the four-zone weather map for the Hawaii Clipper's flight to Midway. All of this having been accomplished, the passengers pulled up in front of the Pan American terminal just before 7:00.

The scene was busy. Boyle was making the last notations on the weather map that he would pass on to the flight crew. Outside, the morning was quiet and the sky was just beginning to brighten. Far in the distance, lights from the battleships anchored at Ford Island were shimmering on the water. Just down the path, gently tugging at its mooring lines, the Hawaii Clipper had been fueled. Two mechanics snapped the cowl flaps shut on number four engine and jumped off the wing onto the dock, completing the last minute mechanical checks.

After a long, uneventful night, everything was happening very quickly. Bewildered by the rush at this early hour, Choy looked about the lounge, hoping someone would tell him what he was supposed to do. French had found a comfortable wicker chair in the corner and was using the delay to catch a few more minutes of sleep. But before he had a chance to settle deeply into the chair, Parker rounded everyone up and led them out to the ship. The hectic pace of the morning had caused Boyle to fall behind and he was only now completing his figures on the Clipper's weight-and-balance schedule.

Anxious to be off with the first light of dawn Terletsky motioned to Walker to hurry. Walker hastily checked Boyle's math and then at a half trot he rushed down the dock and met Terletsky on the bridge. The ground crew, sensing Terletsky's irritation, quickly cast off the mooring lines and set the Clipper adrift. Free of the dock, Terletsky was able to relax, since he still had several minutes before dawn.

Holding the flying boat nearly motionless in midstream, Terletsky waited. Then day spilled over the Pali and across the harbor. As though on cue from the sun, Terletsky pressed the power button. Thundering in the yellow light of dawn, the engines sounded across the harbor. In seconds the Hawaii

Clipper was skittering across the water. Terletsky looked at the instrument panel and then up at the horizon, trying to gauge the ship's progress. The dials were steady. Terletsky listened to the spray as it tapped against the floor, telling him that the boat was skimming the water. Suddenly the sound of the rushing water vanished and Terletsky knew they were off. He firmly pulled back on the control yoke, making a swooping bank to parallel the Waianae Mountains. He followed the range that gave him a natural heading for Kauai, just seventy miles beyond Oahu's Kaena Point.

No sooner did Oahu pass to the stern, than Kauai settled below. Cruising at 9,000 feet, the Clipper had found its long-distance stride, sucking a gallon of fuel every mile. Once past Kauai, the whole world opened up before the ship. Of all the dozens of times Terletsky had flown past Kauai, this moment touched some virgin sense. The engines drummed a well-measured beat. The Clipper, properly trimmed, seemed to float rather than fly. Ahead lay a wonderfully open sky. Below, the radiant blue ocean contrasted sharply with the shallow green water.

On this leg, and on such a startlingly clear day navigation was almost superfluous. From Niihau, the last main island in the Hawaiian chain, dozens of frail atolls and occasional rocky islets directed Terletsky on a straight line to Midway. Like a well-marked highway Nihoa led to Necker Island, then to Gardner Pinnacles, to Laysan Island, and finally to Midway. All through the day, spread out like an abstract form, the sea changed at whim through the blue-green spectrum.

Terletsky glanced to his left. The rising sun glinted off the spinning propellers. It all seemed so serene, so sure.

Ivan Parker parted the curtains that separated the lounge from the galley. "Midway Island, gentlemen." Choy leaned toward the window. Ahead and just off to the right, clearly etched against the deep blue water, two sugar-white atolls appeared in the reflected sunlight.

Through the day John Boyle at Pearl Harbor had maintained regular half-hour radio checks with McCarty. At the halfway point Midway took over, plotting the Hawaii Clipper's course at thirty-minute intervals. This procedure, followed between each base, was instituted so that at least one base would always know the Clippers' positions and the status of the flights at all times.

Thirty miles out, when Terletsky first spotted Midway, McCarty radioed the atoll that they were on their final approach; in turn, the base manager set off a siren, notifying the base that the Clipper would land within minutes. When the siren screamed across the atoll the landing crew rushed out to the lagoon. In the meantime Terletsky had circled around to the northwest for his approach. Once again Choy looked out his window. A few hundred feet below the ocean raced past, then the long even swells were transformed into large white breakers as the barrier reef flashed past. Suddenly, as the hull creased the lagoon, spray shot out from the hull, and tiny rivulets of water streaked across Choy's window.

After settling in the water, the boat glided for several hundred yards. As soon as it slowed, Terletsky turned the Clipper out of the wind and sailed back to the docking float.

It was just 4:22 when the base launch picked up the passengers at the float and took them ashore. At the edge of the lagoon they climbed into a Ford station wagon that drove them to the base hotel.

Once the passengers departed the Clipper the ground crew set out to ready the flying boat for tomorrow's flight. Stored in various sites around the atoll as a fire precaution, gasoline was pumped into 50-gallon drums, loaded aboard sand sleds and pulled across the dunes to the lagoon. There it was put aboard the launch, motored out to the landing float, and finally pumped aboard the Clipper. With the same efficiency as the ground crew, two mechanics climbed up on each wing and started the ritualized overnight service, checking the lubrication and wiring, making minor adjustments, and attending to any details that Cox may have noticed needed correcting on the flight up from Honolulu.

When the passengers pulled up in front of the hotel, two stewards, Chamorros from Guam, dressed in white uniforms with blue piping, greeted them and pointed the way to the lounge. The transition from the Clipper to the hotel was disquieting. Just minutes ago, the steady drone of the engines and the vast Pacific sky had surrounded them. Now, they found themselves in a remarkably modern hotel with dark-skinned stewards attending to their luggage and offering them cocktails. It all seemed so fantastic.

French and Choy asked for old fashioneds while the other four declined cocktails and retired to their rooms to freshen up before dinner. The rooms were Spartan by most standards. Furnished with two twin beds, an electric fan, a dresser, a closet, a telephone for room service, and a vase of fresh flowers, each room also had a private shower that used hot water heated by solar collectors. Basic indeed, but after a long flight and in the middle of the Pacific Ocean, luxury.

Shortly before 7:00 a mellow-toned gong sounded down the halls and then out the front of the hotel, announcing the dinner hour. A source of pride among the kitchen staff, the lavishly prepared dinners were made largely from fresh food. A supply ship called at Midway and Wake every three months, leaving a variety of meats and canned goods, the base gardens produced fresh vegetables, and, as needed, the Clippers flew in supplementary items.

During dinner, French was the first to broach the subject of the fortune Choy was carrying. Everyone was aware that it was a touchy subject and no one, thus far, felt comfortable asking about it. Choy, too, was reluctant to discuss the matter and merely conceded that he was carrying some funds for the Nationalists.

After dinner, Choy and French wandered into the lounge. They asked for drinks and tuned in a late night news program all the way from Hollywood: It had rained for eight straight days in the New York area and many communities were flooded, four men were trapped on a ledge in the Swiss Alps, John Ford was signed to direct Eddie Cantor's new movie, *Mr. Average Man*, and the announcer reported that there were no games scheduled in the Pacific Coast League. The news from China was most disheartening for Choy: Two thousand Japanese shock troops had moved far up the Yangtze River and had landed near Kiukiang, a resort village. At the same time another group of Japanese troops had fought their way to the base of Kuling Mountain near the resort. It appeared that Kuikiang would fall within days. Choy sat quietly through the broadcast but at its conclusion, he almost shouted at French, "That is why I am going to Chungking." French, surprised by Choy's passion, did not respond.

9
Scandal

January 1935

WHILE THE PACIFIC BRISTLED WITH ACTIVITY in early 1935, in New York Juan Trippe found Pan American besieged by a legal whirlwind which threatened to tear the airline apart. For some time the airline industry had been under investigation by the Senate and the Post Office Department for alleged collusion in obtaining mail contracts. In January the Post Office offered Trippe the opportunity to attend a public meeting that would determine whether Pan Am's lucrative mail contracts should be cancelled. This investigation did not come as a surprise to Trippe.

Two years earlier, in the last days of the Hoover administration, James Mead, chairman of the House Post Office Committee, listened to testimony on the government's disposition of mail contracts. At the conclusion of the hearings the Republican-dominated committee found Postmaster General

Walter Brown innocent of any impropriety. A few months later though, the new Democratic administration took power, unconvinced that things had been so innocent.

The new Postmaster General, James. A. Farley, a large jovial Irishman who had previously held various appointed positions in New York and helped catapult Roosevelt into the White House, charged that many mail contracts had been awarded to airlines through collusion and favoritism and so were invalid. Farley believed that the major airlines had been favored over the smaller lines in the Hoover years, and that there was little if any competitive bidding for government contracts. He further charged that on the basis of guaranteed profits from the Post Office Department, some insiders had used the promise of government money to formulate wild, unsound stock promotions for their personal profit. As extensive and potentially devastating as these charges were to the airlines, they rested on a single and somewhat debatable point. Airmail legislation in the 1920s had been written in a manner that tended to consolidate the airlines around the Post Office Department and government money. Through Walter Brown's administration the Post Office paid eight times more for mail than Pan American received on a per-pound basis for passengers. So obviously the airline found it far more attractive to carry mail than people. The Post Office's financial backing of the airlines in turn gave the postmaster general enormous power to determine the course of American commercial aviation.

But curiously, the postmaster general's power rested on two vague phrases in the legislation known as the McNary-Watres Act, which required that the postmaster general award contracts to the "lowest responsible bidder" who best served the "public interest." The meaning of "responsible" and "public interest" was not spelled out. The congressional debate largely turned on these two phrases.

Shortly after Roosevelt took office, the Senate organized the Special Committee on the Investigation of Air Mail and Ocean Mail contracts—later known as the Black Committee after its soft-spoken chairman, Hugo L. Black of Alabama. The investigation unfolded in Room 312 in the old Senate Office Building. On Thursday, September 28, 1933, Black called the hearings to order. The investigation began slowly, but eventually the stories told in Room 312 became some of the hottest news items to come out of Washington in a long time. In the course of the hearings virtually every high-level official even remotely associated with commercial aviation was called to testify. From September 1933 through early 1934 the Committee room sizzled with accusations, denials, and counter accusations.

Though Juan Trippe was not called during the first two years of the investigation, Pan Am had won its contracts in essentially the same manner as the domestic airlines. Pan American was favored beyond all the others, however, receiving preferential treatment as well as financial and political support from several departments, not only the Post Office.

Harry New, a former Indianapolis newspaper publisher and Indiana senator, acted as postmaster general in 1928 and 1929, the most critical years of Pan American's development. Though the Black Committee accused Brown of giving special support to commercial aviation, New really instituted the policies Brown followed. The airmail acts of the mid- and late 1920s bestowed unmitigated power on the postmaster general. The Post Office's generous, ten-year contracts should have been awarded on the basis of competitive bidding, but in reality the lowest bidder did not always receive the contract. During this era Pan American won every mail contract it bid on, even though it was the lowest bidder on only one occasion. How could this have happened?

Pan American won because the Post Office Department

decided, as the McNary-Watres Act allowed, that it best met the needs of the United States and the public interest regardless of the size of its bid. The mail contracts awarded to Trippe in the late 1920s proved so lucrative that Pan Am based much of its subsequent expansion in the Pacific and Atlantic on the financial leverage won through these first contracts. Some of the money Pan Am earned through these contracts came from such twisted legislation that it seemed as though the government was willing to go any distance to support the airline.

Shortly after the inauguration of flights to Cuba, Trippe moved the Pan Am airport back to Miami and opened a small ticket office on Biscayne Boulevard. From the very first day the new office opened PAA agents ballyhooed the flights, reminding the Florida tourists that the bars were open in Havana and that Cuba had all the rum they could drink. Still, flying passengers was a sideline; the real profits were in the mail. Trippe made the move to Miami to increase the distance of the mail route and the size of mail revenues, not for passenger convenience. Not long after Trippe made this move the government comptroller ruled that Pan Am could only be paid for the flight to Havana since the flight back did not carry U.S. mail. New ruled that Pan American could indeed collect for both trips. The Post Office paid Pan Am for the round trips for nearly a year in defiance of the comptroller until Representative Kelly drafted an amendment to his airmail bill which allowed Pan Am to collect legally and retroactively for both trips.

This type of manipulation raised all sorts of questions, but since mail revenues literally meant success or failure to Pan Am, its postal subsidy was never seriously challenged. Postmasters General New and Brown believed that. Pan American's competition originated on the international level. Airlines such as Imperial, Air France, and KLM, which were largely or entirely government subsidized, were seen as Pan

Am's real competitors. They reasoned that in order for Pan American to meet the international competition the government had to support and protect Pan Am. Because of this backing Pan Am grew much faster than the free market would normally have allowed.

Pan American, the government's chosen instrument in international aviation, was a government-sanctioned monopoly. As such it did not have American competitors and expanded as fast and as far as Trippe wanted. After only seven months in business Pan Am added 4,000 miles to its routes in Central America, boosting its postal revenues from $160,000 to over $2.5 million. With dramatic, guaranteed revenue increases such as these Pan American turned itself into one of the hottest items on the stock market, further improving its financial standing.

All of Pan Am's original stock had been privately placed at $15 per share, and each original investor was given a perpetual warrant to buy two shares at $15 for each share held. Soon after October 1928, PAA listed at $35 a share. In 1929, it reached $89.87 and eventually hit $91 later in the year. The potential profits to the insiders were enormous, and many took advantage of their privileged position, selling their shares to the public. Charles Lindbergh, for example, made a quick $150,884.80 on his original warrants. This type of conduct was not uncommon, and to a degree merely reflected the business morality of the times.

Perhaps the most blatant incident of using privileged position and wealth to further enhance personal profit and power occurred in April 1929. Richard Hoyt, hoping to widen his margin of control over Pan American, offered Frederick B. Rentshler, president of United Aircraft and Transportation Corporation, the opportunity to purchase 50,000 shares of Pan Am for $20 less than the open market price.

An early conglomerate, United Aircraft embraced such

prominent aeronautical concerns of the day as Boeing Air-
plane Company, Boeing Air Transport, Pratt & Whitney
Aircraft Company, Chance Voight Corporation, Hamilton
Aero Manufacturing, Stout Air Services, Standard Propeller
Corporation, Northrop Aircraft Corporation, and Sikorsky
Aviation Corporation. Overseeing United, Chairman William
Boeing commanded a board of directors who in turn were also
presidents or highly placed officers of Ford Motor Company,
General Motors, Standard Oil of California, and the National
City Bank of New York. So when Hoyt approached United he
hoped to acquire a formidable ally.

But United also hoped to gain more than a quick profit
from the Pan American stock purchase. On April 5, 1929,
Boeing wired Rentschler agreeing to the purchase and pointing out that United could expect orders for aeronautical equipment from Pan American:

> I think that you will agree with me that Pan
> American, because of its size and because of the
> important contracts they have, is, potentially, the most
> interesting of all the transport lines now established
> with the possible exception of our own Chicago-San
> Francisco. . . . [air route]. . . . They are going to use a
> great deal of equipment. . . .

The combined efforts of these men and the corporations
they represented fashioned an airline unlike any other in the
world. Though Pan American's backers were men of excep-
tional wealth, its wide-ranging success was not entirely based
on financial clout. Trippe and his allies—William Boeing,
Fred Rentschler, Richard Hoyt, W. Averell Harriman, Seymour Knox, and Cornelius Whitney, among others—were
men of privilege, of similar background, they came from the
American aristocracy and could get the things they wanted

from the government. Political power by access to the White House, the Post Office and State Departments is what set Pan American apart from all the other airlines.

In testimony before Senator Black, Boeing revealed part of the reason for Pan Am's unparalleled growth in Latin America:

> Pan American Airways was formed by practically all of the aviation groups and we felt that we should be interested in it. It was at a period when foreign companies were operating in South America under concession and if Pan American did not go in there and did not have the wholehearted support of the whole group, it was felt that the foreign companies would get the better of us there.

Pan American was rarely mentioned in the course of the Senate hearings, but occasionally information like Boeing's statement surfaced. Shortly after 2:15 on the afternoon of February 20, 1934, Senator Black began to pry back the lid that had concealed Pan American's connection with the government. By constructing a complex web of questions and statements about Walter Brown's relationship with Pan Am, Black finally asked Brown point-blank:

> ... Is it not true that during your entire administration when there came up a question as to whether the Pan American Company could get a concession in South America or some other company would get a concession in South America, that you asked the State Department to intervene through its Ambassadors and consuls in favor of the concession to the Pan American Company?

Passengers had to board the Clippers from a landing float in the middle of Midway lagoon. Steward is Ivan Parker. (Pan American World Airways)

Juan Trippe is sitting with Assistant Post Master W. Irving Glover as the bids for the new mail routes to Puerto Rico and Panama are opened. Cornelius Vanderbilt Whitney is standing. (Pan American World Airways)

The S.S. North Haven standing off Midway. Supplies had to be shuttled ashore to Midway and Wake as there were no docking facilities at the two desert islands. (Pan American World Airways)

Captain Edwin Musick at the controls of the Sikorsky S-42 flying boat (Pan American World Airways)

Musick purposefully delayed the landing of the Pan American Clipper by making a wide arc over Diamond Head so that he would arrive exactly on time. (National Archives)

Captain Edwin Musick, in white cap and dark suit, is boarding the Pan American Clipper, a Sikorsky S-42 flying boat, on the day of the first survey flight to Hawaii. (Pan American World Airways)

The Pan American Clipper on its maiden flight to Honolulu (Pan American World Airways)

Japan's "Mavis" seaplane. The Mavis design was virtually identical to Pan American's Sikorsky S-42. (Shin Meiwa Industry Company Limited)

Pan Am's S-42. The American Sikorsky preceded the Imperial navy's Mavis by several years. (Pan American World Airways)

Moored on the Wake lagoon, the Hawaii Clipper is being serviced for the following day's flight to Guam. (Pan American World Airways)

The landing pier at Wake with the gazebo in the foreground (Pan American World Airways)

The lounge in the Wake hotel. The facilities at Wake and Midway were identical. (Pan American World Airways)

The China Clipper in the Alameda lagoon on the morning of its maiden flight to the Far East. (San Francisco Chronicle)

On a publicity flight fifteen miles off San Francisco, Ed Musick spoke to the nation over NBC radio. This and similar events helped build world-wide enthusiasm for the trans-Pacific route. (Pan American World Airways)

Fred Noonan at the navigator's table aboard the Pan American Clipper. (Pan American World Airways)

From the left, the China Clipper's crew as they appeared on the morning of November 23 in Honolulu: Captain Edwin Musick, First Officer R.O.D. Sullivan, Second Officer George King, First Engineer C. D. Wright, Second Engineer V. A. Wright, Radio Operator W. T. Jarboe, and Navigator Fred Noonan. (Pan American World Airways)

Brown replied, "I don't know as to that, but I know that I did on several occasions." Black continued this line of questioning and a few minutes later, Brown expanded on the tripartite relationship between the Post Office Department, the State Department, and Pan American:

> ... I think the State Department finally reached the
> conclusion [that] the United States Government was in
> partnership with the Pan American in a mail service
> to South América ... I suppose the State Department
> did just what I did, tried to make a success of it.

In the face of this unified front it is surprising that anyone even considered challenging Trippe. But one did. In the summer of 1928, Ralph O'Neill, a balding World War I ace, met with the assistant postmaster general, Irving Glover, to discover if the Post Office Department would back an American airline with a mail contract flying the east coast of South America. O'Neill's proposal leapfrogged far beyond Pan Am, which, at the time, flew only as far south as Central America. Glover told O'Neill that federal support was indeed possible.

Shortly afterwards, James Rand of Remington Rand Corporation and several more wealthy backers lined up behind O'Neill's project, the New York, Rio, Buenos Aires Line (NYRBA). Over the months O'Neill worked a near miracle; by early 1929, he had collected mail contracts from Argentina, Uruguay, Brazil, and Chile, purchased flying equipment superior to Pan American's, and received the personal assurance of President Coolidge that he would be allowed to bid on American contracts on an equal footing with Pan American in the future. By the end of 1929, O'Neill had clearly outmaneuvered Trippe, inaugurating the first U.S. air passenger service from New York to South America. In the spring of 1930, it appeared the NYRBA would receive the same kind of financial security as Pan Am when Herbert Hoover again confirmed that O'Neill would be allowed to bid against Trippe. But on the day following Hoover's announcement, Walter Brown contradicted the president, saying that there would be no new mail contracts until certain issues were settled between Pan American and NYRBA.

A former Toledo, Ohio politician, Walter Brown first arrived on the Washington scene with the Coolidge administration. After working with Coolidge for several years, he moved to the Department of Commerce where he worked under Herbert Hoover. Brown watched Hoover with some admiration and after he was appointed chairman of the Republican party he began to promote Hoover as Coolidge's successor. Once Hoover had been elected, he rewarded Brown with the traditional Post Office appointment. By handling the largest budget in the government, deciding which airlines received contracts, and serving as the chairman of his party, in some instances Brown actually wielded more power than Hoover. So when Brown contradicted Hoover and said NYRBA would not obtain a mail contract, it stuck.

Brown wanted O'Neill to sell out to Pan American. Brown succeeded. After months of haggling, with Pan Am in the dominant position, O'Neill finally turned over NYRBA to Trippe for fifty cents on the dollar. On the day after Pan Am assumed control, Brown advertised for bids on the mail route tracing the old NYRBA line to Chile. Without competition, Trippe bid and won the maximum legal rate once more.

Because of contracts such as this, Pan American's profits skyrocketed. Between 1929 and 1933, the years that most concerned the Black Committee, Pan American never realized less than 76 percent of its revenues from the Post Office, once receiving as much as 92 percent. The mail revenues translated into a $23-million subsidy during the toughest days of the Depression.

In spite of the extravagant subsidies and the privileges Pan Am obviously received from Brown, Farley, the airline's arch-critic, did not openly challenge Pan Am; instead he wrote Senator Black, counseling against dragging Trippe into Room 312:

The cancellation of these contracts would not be in the public interest as such action would probably disrupt American service to the Latin American countries and might result in great harm to our trade relations.

Farley wrote a similar letter to Roosevelt:

Either most or all of the contracts under consideration in this report may be cancelled because they were awarded as a result of negotiation and not by competitive bidding as provided by law. It is believed, however, that the cancellation of the contracts would not be in the public interest as such actions would probably disrupt American air service to the Latin American countries and might result in great harm to our trade relations with these countries. There is no other air company in the United States that has the experience, the equipment, the necessary concessions with the Latin American countries and other facilities for service that Pan American Airways System has for operations in this territory. . . .

The State Department also wrote directly to Senator Black on behalf of Pan American:

Pan American is entwined with half the governments of the world and cancellation of its contracts would

severely damage trade relations and the flow of
information through Pan American's unofficial
channels.

The Black Committee did not achieve a clear-cut legal
resolution. Certainly Farley's case was weakened to some
extent because John Mayer, a postal stenographer, burned
twenty-four drawers of Brown's correspondence dealing with
airmail contracts. Nevertheless, after the hearings closed the
Post Office Department cancelled every airmail contract—
except Pan American's. To prevent interlocking directorships,
which had produced several large monopolies, virtually all
high-level airline officials were forced to resign. Many of the
large corporations such as United Aircraft and Transport
Company were broken up into separate manufacturing and
transport companies. The committee also cleaned up the
financial backing of the airlines so that it would no longer be
possible to parlay small investments and guaranteed government mail income into personal multimillion dollar returns.

Pan American eluded the scrutiny of the Black Committee but it did not escape the hearings unscathed. Though
Trippe was offered an opportunity to defend Pan American in
January 1935, nearly a year after the Black Committee
adjourned, he waived his right to attend the aforementioned
meeting that was to determine whether Pan American's contracts should be cancelled along with the domestic airlines.

In the end Trippe's absence made little difference. Congress and the Post Office Department recommended that Pan
Am's contracts be cancelled by 25 percent. But when Trippe
protested, Pan American was finally meted out a puny 10
percent reduction in its postal subsidy.

The money earned from the Post Office for carrying mail
to South America paid for the Martin Clippers and the Pacific
bases. Similarly, the China mail contract, not freight or pas-

senger revenue which remained exceedingly low all through the 1930s, sustained the day to day operations of the trans-Pacific route. The line of bases to China through the Japanese Mandates and later the South Pacific route were projects financed and encouraged by the highest levels of government.

10

Protest

March 1935-April 1935

N<small>O SOONER WAS</small> P<small>AN</small> A<small>MERICAN</small> <small>ASSURED</small> that it would survive the Congressional hearings intact, than Trippe again turned to the Pacific.

The Pacific route was a project of far-reaching proportions and when completed it reshaped America's relationship with other Pacific countries. From the beginning it was decided that the bases would be more than mere commercial way stations. The windy sand dunes of Midway would be transformed into an outer screen that eventually would be capable of protecting Pearl Harbor. Wake, a lonely, rat-infested coral reef, would soon support a sophisticated aeronautical village. Guam, surrounded by the Japanese Mandates and highly vulnerable to invasion, would take the first step toward fortification, and the Philippines would, for the first time, have a speedy, efficient transportation system connecting it with the United States.

Each base from San Francisco to Manila would be a community unto itself. Each would have clear, safe landing areas, a landing float or dock, fuel depots, a powerhouse, and a communications center, in addition to staff quarters for both the ground and flight crews. Once the bases were established, Pan Am would staff each island with technical and nonskilled staffs, which could keep the bases functioning and service up to three flights a week. The island crews would include a base manager, radio operators, mechanics, laborers, cooks, and stewards.

To fashion the coral atolls into modern air bases, André Priester called William Grooch, operations manager of CNAC, back from China to head the construction crew. In California Grooch leased property on the north shore of Alameda, directly across the bay from San Francisco, for the air terminal, then began assembling supplies and hiring laborers at Pier 22 on San Francisco's Embarcadero.

For the cruise Grooch commissioned the S.S. *North Haven* and soon equipment began piling up along the docks. The manifest listed over 108,000 items, totalling 6,000 tons of cargo in all, enough to finish existing facilities at Pearl, Guam, and Manila, and to build two complete villages and air bases at Midway and Wake. The manifest included every conceivable item from spark plugs to toilet bowls—radio gear, dock timbers, household furniture, plumbing and electrical fixtures, five-ton electrical generators, cold-storage plants, refueling equipment, spare aircraft parts. Further, to make the bases self-supporting and reasonably comfortable, Grooch added to the list 110,000 cigarettes, 10 pounds of chewing gum, 65 packages of razor blades, 4 dozen combs, 24 dozen handkerchiefs, 24 dozen pairs of shoelaces, 5 dozen bottles of shaving lotion, 100 cartons of candy bars, 2 windmills, wicker porch furniture, 2 tennis nets, and other items running into hundreds of pages.

In March 1934, while Grooch feverishly worked on the San Francisco Embarcadero, the first Sikorsky S–42, christened the Pan American Clipper, was making a series of test flights off the Florida coast. Trippe had ordered the Sikorsky flying boats at the same time he had purchased the Martins. Though smaller, the S–42 was still a high-performance aircraft which embodied all the speed, safety, and ease of maintenance demanded by Pan American. In the end the design of the S–42 represented the combined efforts of not just Igor Sikorsky but of Trippe, Priester, and Lindbergh as well.

Igor Sikorsky had turned out several other Clippers for Pan Am from his Connecticut plant but they had all been boxy designs laced with external bracing—resembling a flying Brooklyn Bridge. The S–42 was different. Paralleling Glenn Martin's leap forward, the S–42 marked a new era of flying-boat design. Powered by four Pratt & Whitney 750-horsepower engines that were streamlined into the wing, the S–42, in the course of its test flights between April and August 1934, set ten world records in speed, load-carrying ability, and altitude—which made the S–42 the best aircraft of its type in the world. But what really set the S–42 apart was its ability to carry a four-ton payload in its nineteen-ton hull. This was a phenomenal advance that seemed to come out of the pages of science fiction.

Still, for all of this, the S–42 was not enough airplane to transport passengers and freight across the Pacific. In order to carry just enough fuel to make the 2,500-mile flight from San Francisco to Honolulu, the passenger seats of the Sikorsky had to be stripped out and replaced with three huge cylindrical fuel tanks and an accompanying maze of pumps, valves, and fuel lines. When rigged like this, Pan Am's flight crews ghoulishly referred to the S–42 as the "Flying Gas Tank."

However, the S–42 was perfect for the short hops in the Caribbean, and would serve quite adequately as a survey craft exploring the Pacific in preparation for the regular commercial flights. In mid-January 1935, operating as a trans-oceanic flying laboratory, the Pan American Clipper started making long trips out of Miami, simulating flights over the Pacific.

As important as the Pacific island bases were to the navy, the Pan American survey flights over the Caribbean, and later over the Pacific, were of equal value to naval aviation in the 1930s. Trans-oceanic flying, except by occasional stunt pilots, was still much too dangerous to be undertaken on any sort of regular schedule. So over the years Pan Am also passed on an expertise and knowledge of the Pacific skies that could not have been gathered by the navy alone. In the next few years Pan Am would help acquire information about how long-distance flying affected pilots. Pan American taught itself, and then the navy and army, long-distance aerial navigation, and it passed on vital data concerning the weather over the vast, virgin stretches of the Pacific. All of this aided naval aviation as much as the physical presence of the island bases.

Edwin Musick, Pan American's chief pilot, led the exploratory flights and later developed many of the flying techniques used in the Pacific. Second only in popularity to Charles Lindbergh in the mid-1930s, Musick gained his reputation because he approached flying with concern, precision, safety, and intelligence that was unheard of among the headline-grabbing stunt pilots of the era. Musick endured when others faded. Newspaper articles labeled him a stoic, but Musick was not so much lacking in emotion as he was an analytical pilot who flew with the rare insight that only the most meticulous planning had allowed him to reach forty-one years.

This caution, this near-slavery to perfection, was a recently acquired trait, though. In his twenties Musick had been as wild and as carefree as any barnstormer in the country. No doubt his maturity grew from those early experiences. In

1916, he was headlined along the Pacific Coast as "Daredevil Musick." While the war in Europe was expanding and the carnival crowds were demanding more dangerous and realistic stunts from exhibition flyers, Musick responded by creating an "Air Duel" that was supposed to reflect the air battles taking place over the Western Front at the time. On a warm summer evening in 1916, Musick sped over a Venice, California crowd in a series of tight circles and figure 8's while an assistant in the rear seat of his obsolete military biplane fired Roman candles and rockets for him to dodge. Near the end of his routine a rocket shot out of control, tore through the lower right wing and set it on fire. With half of the wing in flames Musick opened the throttle and went into a steep dive, hoping the increased wind speed would blow out the flames. But at thirty feet above the ground his wheels snagged a row of trees and the plane flopped down on its belly. Musick and his assistant, with their clothes on fire, jumped out of the plane just before it exploded. Such flying had been foolishness and Musick knew it. The rocket might have ruptured the fuel tank. It might even have hit him.

After this he ended his career as a stunt flyer and enlisted in the army, then transferred to the Marine Corps, where he taught flying until the war ended. Musick saw no future in military aviation and retired from the marines. In the early 1920s he flew vacationers between New York and Atlantic City for Aeromarine, earning a regular paycheck, and more important, adding to his experience. In 1922, during one of his layovers in New York he met his wife, Cleo, at a dinner party at the Astor Hotel. Because of his inherent shyness she was the first and only woman in his life. After they married, Aeromarine folded and for several years the Musicks struggled on his small and infrequent salaries, first for an airline in Florida, then another based in Philadelphia. In the spring of 1927, Musick began flying for the Reynolds Company, a line ferrying commuters between Haddonfield, New Jersey and New York.

Through the couple's first years together, life as a pilot's wife was not what Cleo considered secure, in spite of Musick's conservative nature. The constant traveling was enough, the perils of flying bothered her even more. One afternoon Cleo drove out to the Haddonfield airport to pick up Musick after his last flight back from New York. Parked near the edge of a runway, she watched several airplanes take off and land for nearly half an hour. Shortly before Musick was due in, the last Reynolds flight of the day to New York sat at the end of the field, warming engines. After a few moments the plane taxied by, picking up speed. Cleo smiled and waved at the passengers. As the liner fought its way into the sky, its motors stopped. The pilot frantically tried to bank the plane back to the right. But only a few hundred feet from where Cleo was parked the plane crashed nose-first and exploded. Horrified, Cleo stared at the roaring flames as they consumed the passengers she had just watched taxi by. She had never seen anything like it but she instantly knew that this could happen to anyone, even Ed. Soon after the accident a lawsuit forced Reynolds out of business.

About the same time, in Florida, André Priester was hiring pilots for the newly organized Pan American Airways. He offered Musick a job. But life was scarcely better with Pan Am for the first few years. The airline's base in Key West was a hot, humid, remote speck on the edge of the Caribbean with no modern conveniences. Fresh water was rationed and everyone had to bathe in brackish well water. There was no refrigeration and the meat in the local store, dotted with flies, had a bluish cast. So the couple's dinners were usually made up of fish Musick caught in the afternoons.

But by 1934 the hardships of starting up the line had passed and the Musicks shared in the success of Pan Am. In anticipation of moving to California, Cleo rented a fashionable apartment in the Crestview Building in San Francisco's posh Pacific Heights.

If life at the bottom had been hard for Musick, then life as Pan Am's premier pilot proved to be more trying. Now, rather than seeking cheering crowds as he did in his youth, he did everything possible to avoid publicity. It was impossible; the press was busy making him a national hero. Advertising agencies tried to entice him to endorse shaving cream and cigarettes. He declined. The public relations department at Pan Am asked him to shave his beard twice daily so that he would photograph better. He did that. He and Cleo vacationed in Manhattan only because he felt that he could lose himself in the crowds. Even at parties among friends Musick rarely uttered a sentence of more than four or five words; usually he quickly retreated to a sofa and sipped a cup of tea. Liquor nauseated him.

Musick's personality was an important ingredient in the promotion of the flights to the Far East. Pan American realized from the outset that promoting the line would be something of a double-edged sword. It had only been seven years since Lindbergh had crossed the Atlantic and, though interest in aviation was at an all-time high, the public's confidence in air travel was still fragile. Pan American's press releases on the Pacific tended to be dry, factual reports so that it would appear that trans-oceanic flying was as safe and commonplace as riding the morning trolley to work. At the same time, though, with over $4 million invested in new aircraft and island facilities, Pan Am had to capitalize on the daring and romance of the Clippers if they were going to insure themselves a steady and enthusiastic interest in the route. Pan American set a careful balance, allowing the romance to speak for itself and using press releases and Musick to reflect their scientific approach to flying. The formula worked, primarily because during the Depression it was impossible for anyone to ignore the wonderful adventure of stepping aboard a luxurious flying boat and speeding off to China. All of the romance and excitement was lost on Musick—the endless stream of banquets and prepared speeches was tedious and distracting.

Every day through March 1935, Musick and his crew flew the S–42 far out into the Caribbean, then spent the evenings studying the blueprints of the Martin Clipper, memorizing its complex engineering details. After weeks of shaking down the S–42, Musick led his crew through a series of flights that were calculated to duplicate every possible problem they might encounter in the Pacific. Flying with different engines dead, then flying by celestial nagivation, and finally navigating by radio bearings, Musick simulated every conceivable misadventure that might occur. In mid-March the S–42 was flying out of Miami over open sea, for twenty hours at a time, simulating the first long hop from San Francisco to Honolulu. Everything had gone according to plan. In one month they would begin survey flights to Hawaii.

As the State Department legal adviser Ralph Hill had predicted, Japan watched the Pan Am line to China with growing concern. On March 14, Japanese naval officers unofficially protested the Pacific project through the Japanese press. The objection reached the front page of *The New York Times*:

JAPAN IS OPPOSED TO PACIFIC LINE

...A Navy Office spokesman, after observing that from a strategic viewpoint he could not criticize Mr. Swanson's action, pointed out that the distinction between commercial airports and those for naval and military use was not clear. The landing places sanctioned could be converted into naval air bases whenever necessary, he said, and although ostensibly intended for commercial use would be a potential danger to Japan because of the proximity of Japan's mandated islands.

Extension of American routes so far into the Western Pacific where the United States possesses no vital commercial interest creates for Japan, said the spokesman, a problem requiring serious consideration.

This was more than a veiled threat and the State Department did not take the protest lightly. Four days after the *Times* article appeared, Trippe met with Stanley K. Hornbeck in Washington. Hornbeck, chief of the State Department's Far Eastern Division, was among the most intellectually gifted men in the department. A former Rhodes Scholar, he was born in China and lectured at Harvard on the history of the Far East until he joined the State Department in 1928. This meeting, the first between Trippe and Hornbeck, opened a long-term relationship, which Trippe used to advise and seek advice from the State Department on Pan Am's plans or problems in the Pacific and China.

Deeply concerned with Japan's image of the trans-Pacific route, Hornbeck wanted to temper the militaristic complexion of the route by offering Japan landing privileges at Guam. Trippe agreed in principle with Hornbeck's plan. Hornbeck passed the idea around to various executive departments and everyone, including the navy, agreed that the offer should be made to Japan. By April Cordell Hull initialed the idea and forwarded it to Roosevelt who, in turn, approved the plan.

But the idea withered from neglect. For all the intensity and concern Hornbeck's plan received, no one seemed interested or concerned enough to take the initiative to put the idea into action.

Though the navy considered the mid-Pacific route a valuable part of the national defense and desperately wanted air bases on the islands west of Oahu, it was not happy with Pan American's use of Pearl Harbor. In 1935, Clarence Young, Pan Am's western representative, searched throughout Oahu for a base that would be both convenient to Honolulu and a safe harbor for the Clippers. The navy suggested Pan American use Kaneohe Bay on the windward side of Oahu, but Young pressed hard for the more convenient landing area at Pearl Harbor. Reluctantly, the navy agreed, but only because it considered the route as a whole essential to the development of its Pacific strategy. The commandant of the Fourteenth Naval District, Admiral Harry E. Yarnell, wrote the first favorable report on Young's request:

> . . .As it is believed that the operating bases to be established by this company in Midway, Wake Island, Guam and Manila are of great advantage to the Navy, it is believed that the request of the Pan American Company to use the waters of Pearl Harbor, if other areas prove unavailable or unsuitable, should receive the favorable consideration of the Navy.

A few weeks later on May 15, Admiral Ernest J. King, chief of the Bureau of Aeronautics, had the final word:

> . . . The requirements of Pan American Airways for a seaplane operating area are practically identical with the Navy requirements for an auxiliary operating area. These two developments should go hand in hand. . . .

For these reasons Pan American must have had little doubt that the navy would eventually grant it landing rights in Pearl Harbor. In April 1935, while Young dickered with the navy, Ed Musick in California prepared to make the first of several survey flights to Pearl Harbor. Through the first months of training in Florida and later along the California coast, Musick's greatest concern, other than the weather, was the accuracy of the radio direction finder. At sea, the navigator could plot the course in the general direction of the base by celestial bearings, but in order to achieve consistent pinpoint accuracy in and out of the bases the radio direction finder was absolutely vital. Pan American solved the navigation problem well before the first series of survey flights to Hawaii. But the uncertainties of the weather were not as quickly understood.

The sky above the Pacific was still wilderness in 1935. Musick knew that nothing—not the direction finder, certainly not the Clippers' four powerful engines, not his twenty years of experience—could save the flying boats from the fury of the Pacific typhoons. Over the next few months it would be Musick's duty to chart the Pacific and create a safe system for the succeeding flights to follow.

For weeks prior to the first survey flight Musick and Bill Clover, the chief weather forecaster at the Alameda base, pored over the weather charts trying to develop a reliable forecasting method that would guarantee the safety of the trans-Pacific flights. While employed by the domestic airlines, Clover used the air-mass-analysis method of weather forecasting, in which he relied on spot weather reports from around the country to make up his prediction. But the problem was vastly more complicated over the Pacific. In constructing a Pacific weather profile Clover would have to rely on few and widely scattered reports from ships and the island bases. So Musick knew that on occasion the forecasts would be inaccurate, that any given flight might meet unexpectedly violent weather and be forced to turn back. It was a built-in risk.

On April 16 at 3:45 P.M., Musick gunned the Pan American Clipper's four Hornet engines and departed San Francisco for the first survey flight to Pearl Harbor. The following morning he arrived over Diamond Head a few minutes ahead of schedule. In order to keep the flight on time he banked the ship into a wide arc over Waikiki, delaying the landing just long enough so that he touched down after the predicted 18-hour, 37-minute flying time. A week later the Pan American Clipper returned to the Alameda base. On the same afternoon that the Clipper took off a Japanese daily newspaper, the Harbin *Nichi Nichi*, speculated on the purpose of the trans-Pacific line:

The American airboat which left Alameda on April 16, arrived safely at Pearl Harbor the next morning, covering 2,400 miles and carrying 15,000 letters. This success naturally makes us think of the second section of the American scheme, from Manila to Canton. It hardly needs to be said that the opening of regular flights between America and China greatly affects Japan's strategic situation. Even if the route is restricted to commercial flights, who can assure that it would not be used for military purposes in case of emergency? If we view this effort in terms of the large sacrifice America has been and still is making for the success of the flight between San Francisco and Hawaii, it looks like the line has a military purpose. If it is declared experimental or simply commercial, that is because America is afraid of violating the nonarmament provisions of the Washington Treaty in the Pacific. Finally, if China permits the American-Chinese air route, Japan must demand a Japanese-Chinese route, connecting Fukuoka and Shanghai or north China and Manchuria. Britain will surely follow suit. The depth of the American concern

in the Far East can be measured by this scheme, to say
nothing of her naval maneuvers which are to take
place only a few hundred miles off our Kurile Islands
early next month.

The manner in which this protest was levied said as much
about the Pacific masquerade as did its content. This and all
other condemnations of Pan American's project were submitted through newspaper editorials, never through official channels. Japan did this to protect itself from American counter-
protests, because it too was building commercial facilities in
Micronesia that had military ramifications.

Prior to Japan's resignation from the League of Nations
in 1933, the Imperial navy adhered to the letter of the nonfortification provisions of the League Mandate and the Washington Treaty. After 1933, though, Nanyo Kohasta Kaisha, the
South Seas Development Corporation, fronted for the Imperial navy. At first building commercial facilities and later more
ambitious projects in Micronesia, the South Seas corporation
lent the construction program a commercial flavor. As time
passed the building went far beyond what anyone would call
normal civilian expansion.

The Aslito airfield, along with seaplane ramps, communication facilities, and a general harbor expansion, eventually
turned Saipan into the Imperial navy's central headquarters in
Micronesia. In 1937, a secret seaplane base was built at Koror
in the western Palaus and in time Truk, Ponape, Tinian, and
Pagan were developed similarly to Saipan and became major
Japanese fortresses. In order to protect themselves from coun-
teraccusations, and possibly demands for on-site investigations, Japan's criticism of Pan American always appeared
only in harshly worded newspaper editorials.

11

Espionage

May 1935

THOUGH YOUNG HAD SECURED THE USE OF PEARL HARBOR and Grooch had nearly completed the Pacific bases in May 1935, Trippe still had not acquired landing rights on the China coast. Through most of the spring, Trippe had talked with British officials about securing rights in Hong Kong, but with no success. Then, in the beginning of May, London inexplicably reversed itself and through the State Department offered Trippe the opportunity to apply for landing privileges into Hong Kong.

On May 8, Trippe wrote to both London and Washington as suggested. But unknown to him, the British had planted a hook in the Hong Kong application process. Once Trippe applied for rights through the American State Department, negotiations would leave the realm of business and become an official matter between the U.S. and U.K. governments. The

British knew that this would remove Trippe from the negotiations and that they would then be in a position to demand reciprocal landing rights from the United States elsewhere in the Pacific. It was a shrewd move, calculated to strip Trippe of his authority in the bargaining process. Unaware of what lay ahead, Trippe submitted Pan Am's application through Cordell Hull.

But just two weeks later Trippe uncovered some information that made him suspicious of Britain's generosity. On May 24 he visited Assistant Secretary of State R. Walton Moore to exchange a few thoughts, then walked down the hall and met with Richard Southgate, chief of the Division of International Conferences. Trippe told Southgate that he had discovered some surprising information. According to Southgate:

> He stated that he had learned that in the event the Department should request permission for PAA to fly into Hong Kong the British would request permission for Imperial Airways to fly into the Philippine Islands. . . . Recently a number of British Royal Flying Corps airplanes had made a visit to the Philippines. He said that almost the entire personnel of the crews of these ships were Imperial Airways men and that the purpose of the flight, although called a military visit, was to survey the feasibility of Imperial Airways entering the Philippine Islands. . . .

Trippe asked Southgate to hold on to his Hong Kong application for the time being. Actually, he said, Hong Kong was only a port of convenience. He chatted further about the Hong Kong problem for several minutes, and then flabbergasted Southgate by telling him that he really did not need Hong Kong because he had secretly acquired rights into Macao. This put him in a very strong bargaining position with

the British and the State Department. Trippe did not hesitate
to use this position, and his value to the military, to try to bag
additional financial backing from the government:

> . . . Mr. Trippe also indicated that Imperial Airways
> are tripling their capital and that Air France is taking
> similar steps. He also dwelt on the military aspects of
> the situation both in Europe and in the Far East and
> the close relationship which civil aviation would have
> with military aviation in any future wars. Japan,
> Great Britain, France, Italy and Germany all subsidize
> and give definite Government support to their
> international aviation companies. Pan American
> Airways, Mr. Trippe stated, will require aid from the
> American Government if it is successfully to meet this
> competition.

Some time later in the summer, Trippe once again
talked to Hornbeck of the Far Eastern Division about turning Guam into an international base. Everyone, even Hornbeck, had cooled on the idea in the recent months; still,
Hornbeck thought the concept worth pursuing. He suggested that in addition to offering Japan landing rights,
Britain, China, and the Netherlands might be included in
the plan. Obviously the idea of sharing Guam with four
other airlines did not appeal to Trippe and he bluntly
turned down the idea as unworkable:

> . . . He said that hostile criticism in the Japanese press
> had disappeared and he thinks the latent suspicion that
> the Pan American enterprise is a cloak for military
> plans will gradually be reduced to approximate
> negligibility. Mr. Trippe said that Japan is far behind
> Pan American in preparedness to make long

transoceanic flights and that one effect of an offer to
them of privileges at Guam, if made, would be to
cause them to hasten their efforts and thus to bring
nearer the moment when they might ask for more than
that. . . .

Trippe had a very good reason to be concerned about the
state of Japanese aeronautical technology. In the 1930s, Pan
American's long-distance equipment was far superior to that
of any other airline in the world, and even of the navy's. This
meant that Pan Am could fly places others could not and gave
Pan Am a distinct competitive advantage around the world.
Still, it was impossible to contain Pan American's technology
within the limits of commercial aviation or the United
States—some spilled over into the military and some of its
technology crossed international borders.

Though Japanese aircraft manufacturers built good,
small aircraft in the mid-1930s they demonstrated some difficulty in producing large, long-distance aircraft. In the 1930s
many of the best Japanese aeronautical designs were, in fact,
not of Japanese origin at all but based on plans licensed to
Japanese manufacturers generally from Great Britain or the
United States. One clear example, the Nakajima Douglas
DC–2, bears a striking resemblance to the DC–2 simply
because it was built through a license supplied by the American manufacturer, Douglas Aircraft. In the late 1930s and
early 1940s, Japan began to produce aircraft based less and
less on foreign designs, but this practice did not entirely die out
until World War II started.

A notable exception to this practice was the designs of
Pan American's flying boats. So advanced were Pan American's aircraft, specifically the S–42 and the Martin, that the
navy, fearing the loss of America's finest aeronautical technology to Japan, refused to allow the release of these designs.

In late 1933, the Imperial navy, reflecting the rise of Japanese nationalism, requested Kawanishi Aircraft Company, based at Naruo, Japan, to design and build a four-engined flying boat. In the past Kawanishi had had only moderate success in building even small, single-engined amphibians. In early 1934, Kawanishi had begun the design of the flying boat which it designated H6K, later code-named "Mavis" by the Allies.

On the surface, the Mavis, in size and capability, appeared to be a quantum leap forward by Japan, but through the course of its design, Japanese naval officers and civilian engineers displayed an unusually keen interest in Pan American's S-42. Japanese attempts to inspect the S-42 became so brazen that on May 22, 1935, about midpoint in Mavis's design, the Office of Naval Intelligence wrote to Trippe warning him about the Imperial navy's curiosity:

On granting permission for a visit by Engineer Captain T. Sakurai, I.J.N., accompanied by a party of Japanese Naval officers and civilian engineers to the Sikorsky Aviation Corporation at Bridgeport, Conn., on May 17, 1935, the Navy Department specified that these foreigners should not be shown the Type S-42 Flying Boat.

It is possible, that having been denied a view of the S-42 at the factory, the above persons may approach you for authority to inspect a plane of this type after delivery. If such a request is made the Navy Department desires that it be refused.

Fourteen months later Kawanishi ran the first prototype of the Mavis through its air and sea trials. Though slightly larger, the Mavis was virtually a mirror image of the S-42. The Mavis shared feature upon feature with the Pan American flying boat. Both used four engines and American-designed Hamilton three-bladed standard-speed propellers. Both were of all-metal construction except for fabric covering on their control surfaces. The wings of both flying boats were of a high, externally braced, parasol-type construction. The Mavis and the S-42 employed twin tail fins that were supported on an externally braced tail wing. The hull of each, the single most crucial element in seaplane design, was long and low, and each had a characteristically unique pointed bow. These were not casual similarities, nor could they have been the product of unrelated simultaneous development. The S-42, which led the way with these features by nearly three years, appears to be the prototype that Kawanishi used for the Mavis. The variations between the two boats were minor and could be attributed to the two-year difference in their design dates and the subsequent advances in worldwide technology.

The Imperial navy in all likelihood procured specifications for the S-42 from two distinct sources. Several American aeronautical journals published simple engineering monographs on the Sikorsky in 1935. Certainly the Imperial navy, with little difficulty, could have gleaned valuable information from openly published articles.

The second method could have supplied vital first-hand knowledge about the flying boat.

From January through August 1936, a series of confidential reports from the Office of Naval Intelligence crossed Stanley Hornbeck's desk. Each of the reports informed Hornbeck that espionage agents, traced to the Japanese naval attaché's office in Washington, had been seen photographing naval installations along the U.S. south and west coasts.

This was a serious matter and one that caused some friction within the government. An intra-State Department newsletter in July 1936 capsulized the problem, ". . . The State Department and the Navy Department are about ready to come to blows over the question of whether or not we should make public information concerning espionage activities of Japanese in the United States."

In light of Captain Sakurai's request to see the S–42 in May 1935 and Japanese espionage activity on the West Coast, Kawanishi probably received data about the S–42 from agents assigned to the attaché's office.

For all the work and time spent on the Mavis, it was not a notable flying boat. Primarily intended as a long-range reconnaissance bomber, the Mavis actually had a very poor payload carrying capability and, at best, represented a sort of intermediate step between the S–42 and the Martin Clipper. Shortly after the Mavis completed its air trials, the Imperial navy, somewhat dissatisfied with the boat, asked Kawanishi to design yet another seaplane. Designated H8K, code-named "Emily", the Imperial navy's second long-range flying boat entered design in June 1938.

The Imperial navy envisioned the Emily as a jump ahead—as a finer, more powerful seaplane than the Mavis. But there must have been doubts that it could be built. Kawanishi had had only mediocre success with the Mavis, and without outside help the navy was not confident that the Emily would meet its expectations.

In July 1938, with the Emily entering its second month of design, the Imperial navy set out to expedite its design in any manner it could.

12

Wake

July 27, 1938

RIGHT ON TIME, at 7:19 A.M., the Hawaii Clipper roared out of the Midway lagoon.

One hundred-eighty miles out, the Clipper crossed the international date line and with a humor he had practiced on all his previous Pacific crossings, Parker announced, "Gentlemen, today is tomorrow. Set your calendars ahead one day; it is July 27, 1938." The moment was always good for a laugh and some light banter about losing a day in your life. To help the morning pass a little more quickly, Terletsky came back into the lounge and passed out a blue-and-gold dateline certificate that declared the passengers subjects of the sun, moon, and heavens.

In mid-afternoon Meier retrieved his air hook. Like the date line ceremony, this too was a pleasant amusement and it gave Fred Meier an opportunity to explain his work. After graduating from Harvard in 1917, he was appointed the principal plant pathologist with the Agriculture Department's Bureau of Plant Industry in Washington and then, in 1934, was promoted to senior scientist in the Department of Agriculture. While he assembled the air hook, Meier explained that he had been working on the problem of the dissemination of microorganisms in the upper atmosphere since 1927.

Meier collected samples for nearly another hour. Just as he was storing his equipment Parker called Wake Island.

Other than the landing pier at Wake, the facilities at Midway and Wake were identical. The mood, though, was entirely different at Wake—it was something that everyone sensed but would have been hard-pressed to define. Perhaps it was the stark isolation of the atoll. Standing just twenty-eight feet above the sea and hundreds of miles from the nearest land, Wake inspired a sense of loneliness that seemed not altogether unpleasant but still somehow foreboding.

The sea around Wake is very deep and falls away quickly from the atoll. From the air the contrast is thrilling. The shallow green lagoon cuts sharply against the surrounding indigo sea. The sun was high as the Hawaii Clipper drifted into the lagoon. Thousands of shrieking terns scattered as the Clipper's hull touched the glassy water; just as many brightly colored fish darted frantically out of the path of the ship.

Still not yet 4:00 when they landed, there remained enough light to spend a few hours enjoying the island. The Clipper's crew sailed out on the lagoon to do a little sport fishing while several of the passengers took a glass-bottomed boat ride.

After dinner, the passengers and the crew broke off into small groups. Wyman, Kennedy, and Terletsky continued their conversation about aviation and their experiences with Pan American while the Chamorros cleared the dining room. Most of the crew retired to their quarters. French, Meier, Earl

McKinley, and Choy walked out to the gazebo on the land side of the docking pier. Over the years this had become a favorite spot to spend the evenings. A radio operator had installed a speaker connected to the base radio, which played Hawaiian music picked up all the way from KGMB in Honolulu. The air was warm, a light breeze blew in from the sea, and when Choy looked up he said it was frightening to imagine how large the sky was.

13

First Flight

November 1935-January 1936

SEEMINGLY IN DEFIANCE of the approaching storm season, Juan Trippe chose November 22 to open the trans-Pacific line. Like clockwork, winter rains begin, first gently in mid-October, and then by mid-November from Point Sur north a primordial display of hard gray clouds sweeps across San Francisco. In late November, the storm season builds in intensity, not subsiding until March. It is by far the most beautiful but threatening season in the Pacific. But this morning dawned crisp and clear. As Musick looked out his kitchen window toward the Golden Gate he saw blue sky.

Musick had not had a good night's rest although he had slept later than usual. He fumbled with his cigarettes and stirred a spoonful of sugar into his coffee. Thirteen cigarettes, thirteen matches. That was perfect. Twenty cigarettes in a package corresponded perfectly to the twenty matches in a book. Therefore, he never offered a light to anyone until he had lit his own cigarette first. That way he always maintained an equal ratio of cigarettes to matches. It was an idiosyncrasy, and made perfect sense on long flights, where matches were at a premium.

On the previous afternoon Juan Trippe had arrived in San Francisco from the home office in New York. It was his responsibility to make the final decision whether the flight could proceed safely and if so, lead the pre-flight ceremonies. Though everything conceivable had been done, Trippe still had lingering thoughts that things could be more perfect. On the evening of the 21st Trippe questioned his mechanics, engineers, and Musick in his room at the St. Francis Hotel until early the following morning. At the end of the meeting Trippe agreed that they were as ready as they would ever be, and reminded them to get a good night's rest.

Musick worried about the pre-flight ceremonies. He knew the press would be there asking endless questions:

"Captain Musick, how long will your flight be to Honolulu?"

"We've calculated seventeen hours flying time."

"Sir, how long have you been flying?"

"Since I was sixteen."

Perhaps there would be embarrassing questions, too:

"Captain Musick, several Japanese newspapers are saying that Pan American's route to the Far East is really a military operation. Do you have any comments?"

If Musick worried about this question, he should not have. The American press was not looking for that kind of information. The story they wanted was the adventure of the flight, and whatever international importance they attached to the route was only its meaning to business and the inevitable expansion of U.S. trade in the Orient. But while the American press ignored the real story, the Japanese did not. Just days before the China Clipper's maiden flight, another editorial protest appeared in Japan:

> This project can be regarded as military preparations in the guise of civilian enterprise. Commercially and industrially there is no justification for extension of American airways to the Pacific Islands.
>
> Since the projected routes are close to Japan's Mandated Islands, we must give this project serious consideration. The fact permits were issued by the Navy Department strongly suggests the future use of these airports for military purposes is contemplated.

These protests were fruitless and only elicited equally strenuous denials from the United States. So on this morning Japan decided to take direct action against Pan American.

While Musick smoked his cigarette, across the bay two Japanese nationals secretly slipped aboard the China Clipper. The base was largely deserted. The Japanese swiftly oriented themselves in the small chart room and quickly set out to sabotage the radio direction finder. This was one of the trans-Pacific line's most vulnerable points. Keenly aware that the public's faith in Pan Am's ability to span the Pacific was fragile, the Japanese agents were trying to miscalibrate the direction finder. By relying on the improperly functioning navigational instrument for the last few hundred miles out of Honolulu, Musick would become temporarily lost—a horrifying prospect over the vast Pacific Ocean. Japan reasoned that this error on the China Clipper's maiden flight would compromise Pan American's image and call into question the safety of the six-day flights to the Far East. The inauguration of the route would then be postponed, maybe for years, and thus thwart the American Pacific program.

Even before they opened their tool case, the two froze when a voice from behind them shouted, "FBI." The pair was handcuffed and hustled into a dark sedan so quickly that no one, not even the news reporters, knew what had happened.

The arrest, a potentially embarrassing matter to the United States, was not reported because it would have ruined both Pan American's and the navy's plans in the Pacific. Pan Am had spent much of 1935 nurturing its image and the public, though infatuated with the Clippers, was still wary of flying the oceans. Public disclosure of the attempted sabotage would have destroyed what confidence Pan American had laboriously built up over the recent months.

But disclosure would have done far more than damage Pan American; it would have raised a series of embarrassing questions. What was the navy's interest in Pan American and the line to China? Why did the navy ask for jurisdiction over Wake? What was the real purpose of William Miller's expedition to the South Pacific? And why was Pan American so generously subsidized while the country was in the throes of the Depression? Pan American, the FBI, and the navy knew that all of this was better left unanswered.

Anyone who could planned to take the afternoon off and ride the ferry from San Francisco to Alameda to see the China Clipper. By mid-afternoon 25,000 people were gathered at the base. Along the north shore of San Francisco, from the Embarcadero west to the hills near the southern tower of the Golden Gate Bridge, 125,000 more lined up to watch the Clipper make its first flight to the Far East.

The China Clipper was scheduled to take off at 3:45 P.M.. At 2:45 the pre-flight ceremonies began. Millions around the world— in Europe, Japan, South America, the Philippines, and Australia—snapped on their radios, tuned in the signal and leaned forward to hear the broadcast of the China Clipper's maiden flight:

We are here on the shores of historic old San Francisco Bay, on the marine ramp of Pan American Airways' Pacific operating base. Around us surges a great crowd of interested, excited people, extending as far back over the airport as the eye can reach. Above their heads, in the bright sunshine, wave four flags—the territorial flag of Hawaii; the red and blue banner of the newly inaugurated Commonwealth of the Philippines; the flag of the Postmaster General of the United States; and the Stars and Stripes . . .

In a few minutes, now, we will bring to you the sailing of the first "China Clipper" in eighty years, from this grand old Bay from which the original Clipper Ships set sail; we realize that, since time began, this vast Pacific Ocean at our feet stood as an unconquerable barrier between the East and the West. Now, at long last, this barrier is to be no more.

And it is America, whose dynamic energy and courage to pioneer, whose aeronautical genius, whose far-sighted government, has alone of all nations on the face of the earth, made this tremendous achievement possible. Within a few feet of our platform, the China Clipper, studded with powerful engines, her great glistening whale-like hull resting gently in the water, stands ready.

What drama is packed into the hold of this tremendous airliner, the largest ever developed in America where the airplane was born, the most outstanding aircraft ever developed in the world. . .

Now—there are those gathered here to express, in the name of the people of America, the hopes that are

bound up in this amazing service which is about to
begin.

It was as though the first pioneer were about to make the
long trek from Missouri to California. The China Clipper, for
all of those trapped by the Depression, was an image of
American pioneering know-how—an adventure in which
everyone could participate by listening to the radio. The
speeches that followed reflected the optimism that the Clippers
symbolized. The radio announcer continued:

On the wings of these sturdy Clipper ships are pinned
the hopes of American's commerce for a rightful
standing in the teeming markets of the Orient. In no
other section of the United States is that feeling more
keen than here on the Pacific coast, the Orient's
nearest neighbor.

Dignitaries lined up six deep to speak to the world and to
express their enthusiasm and hopes. James Farley first read a
letter from Franklin Roosevelt:

. . . Even at this distance I thrill to the wonder of
it all.
They tell me that the inauguration of the
trans-Pacific sky mail also celebrates the hundredth
anniversary of the arrival of the first clipper ship in
San Francisco. The years between the two events mark
a century of progress that is without parallel, and it is
our just pride that America and Americans have
played no minor part in the blazing of new trails.
There can be no higher hope than that this heritage of
courage, daring, initiative and enterprise will be
conserved and intensified.

Farley paused for a moment, shuffled his papers, and then read his own speech:

Very soon super-planes flying over this route will be transporting passengers and express. A person or letter will arrive in China within six days after leaving New York. This is, indeed, an epoch-making achievement and one which rivals the vivid imagination of Jules Verne.

It has been the experience of the United States that when better communications and faster transportation have been established between this and other countries better understandings have resulted and an improvement in trade and commerce has followed. Therefore, I anticipate that our friendly relations and our commerce with the countries of the Orient will be strengthened and stimulated by the trans-Pacific air mail service.

After Farley concluded his speech, the radio announcer broke in:

All eyes now are on the China Clipper, riding at anchor just beyond our platform. What a thrilling sight she is. So confident, so sturdy. Her gleaming hull and wings glistening in the sunshine, her great engines ready to speed her on her way.

Along a catwalk, now, seven uniformed figures— in navy blue, with white visored caps—Pan American's colors—are moving along the narrow catwalk to the front hatch of the great airliner. There is little excitement about them. They are the flight officers of the China Clipper—winged pioneers about to set out on an ocean's conquest. I want to try, in a

short minute here, to give you their names as they go
aboard. In just a minute, now, the China Clipper will
move to her mooring and await the order to cast off.
Here they are:

The first to go aboard is R.O.D. Sullivan, who, as
the first officer, made the first flights to Hawaii and
Midway islands and, as captain of the Pan American
Clipper, made the initial flights to Wake Island and
Guam. Captain Sullivan is the first officer of the
China Clipper. Right behind him is another old
timer—a product of the old square-riggers and veteran
of all Pan American's Pacific flights—Fred Noonan,
navigation officer of the China Clipper. Now George
King, ocean pilot in training on his first actual Pacific
crossing. He is second officer. Certainly, the China
Clipper can't go wrong in the engineering department.
Both the engineering officers, now going aboard, are
Wright! First Engineering Officer C. D. Wright and
Second Engineering Officer Victor Wright. They are
not brothers, by the way. Right behind them goes
William Jarboe, Jr., radio officer, another veteran of
the Pacific survey flights. The last to go aboard is Pan
American's veteran Edwin C. Musick, captain of the
China Clipper.

President Manuel Quezon of the Philippines spoke over
the radio hookup, followed by the governors of Hawaii and
California, Joseph Poindexter and Frank Merriam, Assistant
Postmaster General Harlee Branch and California's Senator
William McAdoo. Then each of the bases from Hawaii to
Manila tapped out the same message one after the other, "Pan
American Airways trans-Pacific Air Terminal, ready and
standing by." Trippe stepped to the microphone: "Captain
Musick, you have your sailing orders. Cast off and depart for

The China Clipper over the Golden Gate on the afternoon of November 22, 1935. Passengers were not carried aboard the three Martin Clippers until October 1936. (Pan American World Airways)

Upon her arrival in Honolulu in March 1937, Amelia Earhart is flanked by Paul Mantz, her technical advisor, on the left and Fred Noonan, her navigator, on the right. (San Francisco Public Library)

Pan Am's ticket office in the Cathay Hotel was heavily damaged during the Japanese invasion of Shanghai in August 1937. Thousands were killed in the nearby streets. (Pan American World Airways)

Juan Trippe in the late 1930s (Fabian Bachrach)

The China Clipper above San Francisco on a return flight from the Far East (Pan American World Airways)

Overnight servicing at each of the islands insured that the Clippers were in perfect condition for each leg of the trans-Pacific journey. (Pan American World Airways)

The sweeping lines of the Martin Clippers made them the most graceful aircraft in the skies. (San Francisco Public Library)

On the far left is Pan Am's Guam terminal building. The dark building on the far right is the hangar where the Clippers were stored for the evening. (Pan American World Airways)

This is the view Ivan Parker would have commanded when he looked from the galley through the lounge toward the aft storage compartment. There were just six passengers aboard the *Hawaii Clipper* on the afternoon of July 29. (Pan American World Airways)

On the bridge of the Martin Clipper, the Captain sat on the left, the First Officer on the right, and the Radio Operator directly behind the First Officer. (Pan American World Airways)

From 1935 through early 1939, the Martin Clipper was considered the finest flying boat in the world. Some believed that it was the best of any type of aircraft in the skies. (Pan American World Airways)

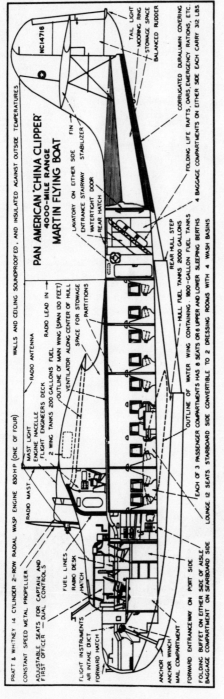

PRATT & WHITNEY 14 CYLINDER 2-ROW RADIAL WASP ENGINE 830 H.P. (ONE OF FOUR)

CONSTANT SPEED METAL PROPELLER

WALLS AND CEILING SOUNDPROOFED, AND INSULATED AGAINST OUTSIDE TEMPERATURES

ADJUSTABLE SEATS FOR CAPTAIN AND
FIRST OFFICER — DUAL CONTROLS

FUEL LINES
RADIO DESK

FLIGHT INSTRUMENTS
AIR INTAKE DUCT
FORWARD HATCH

MAST LIGHT
ENGINE NACELLE
FLIGHT ENGINEERS DECK

RADIO MAST
RADIO ANTENNA

2 WING TANKS 200 GALLONS FUEL
OUTLINE OF MAIN WING (SPAN 130 FEET)
VENTILATOR ALONG CENTER OF HULL

RADIO LEAD IN

SPACE FOR STOWAGE
PARTITIONS

NC14716

TAIL LIGHT
MOORING RING
STOWAGE SPACE
BALANCED RUDDER

FIN
STABILIZER

LAVATORY ON EITHER SIDE
ENTRANCE STAIRWAY
WATERTIGHT DOOR
REAR HATCH

CORRUGATED DURALUMIN COVERING

FOLDING LIFE RAFTS, OARS, EMERGENCY RATIONS, ETC.

4 BAGGAGE COMPARTMENTS ON EITHER SIDE EACH CARRY 3½ TONS

PAN AMERICAN 'CHINA CLIPPER'
4000-MILE RANGE
MARTIN FLYING BOAT

ANCHOR
ANCHOR WINCH
MAIL COMPARTMENT

FORWARD ENTRANCEWAY ON PORT SIDE

FOLDING BUFFET ON EITHER SIDE OF AISLE
BAGGAGE COMPARTMENT ON SEABOARD SIDE

EACH OF 3 PASSENGER COMPARTMENTS HAS 8 SEATS OR 6 UPPER AND LOWER SLEEPING BERTHS
LOUNGE 12 SEATS STARBOARD SIDE CONVERTIBLE TO 2 DRESSING ROOMS WITH 4 WASH BASINS

OUTLINE OF WATER WING CONTAINING 1800-GALLON FUEL TANKS

HULL FUEL TANKS 2000 GALLONS

REAR HULL STEP

Profile of the Martin flying boat. By 1938, the galley was moved next to the
lounge and a crew's quarters installed behind the bridge. The storage compartment extends from the rear hatch to the tail. (San Francisco Public Library)

The Imperial navy's "Emily" duplicated many features of the Martin Clipper. (Shin Meiwa Industry Company Limited)

Specifications for the Emily were developed by the Imperial navy and supplied to Kawanishi Aircraft. (Shin Meiwa Industry Company Limited)

Manila in accordance therewith." The band struck up "The Star Spangled Banner" and as Musick taxied into the Bay the crowd broke into a spontaneous cheer.

Six days later, after 63 hours 24 minutes flying time covering 8,201 miles, the China Clipper splashed into the bay at Manila. The first flight was all that anyone could have hoped for. When asked about the long flight, Musick simply replied, "Without incident." That was exactly what Trippe wanted—simple, straightforward, and without incident.

Although the flight to Manila came off as planned there was still no getting away from the war in China. On the third day of the China Clipper's maiden flight, a CNAC transport en route from Hong Kong to Tientsin was intercepted by two Japanese fighters and forced down. Apparently part of a well-organized plan, the downed transport was immediately surrounded by Japanese troops with fixed bayonets. Two Japanese officers boarded the airplane and accused the passengers and the American captain of spying and photographing Japanese troop movements from the air. The CNAC liner was held for only a few hours but the point had been made: Japan was not happy with CNAC's flights. CNAC flew as much at the pleasure of Japan as of China.

Over the next two months, one storm followed another, forcing each succeeding flight back to California. In the course of these storms an incident occurred; some believe it was the second case of Japanese sabotage at Alameda. On the morning of January 5, 1936, Captain Sullivan made a short three-hour test flight in the China Clipper over San Francisco Bay. The flight proved satisfactory so the operations officer scheduled Sullivan and the China Clipper for an afternoon departure to Honolulu. Sullivan hoped to leave at 4:00 but a fueling problem delayed the flight for nearly an hour. At 4:50, as Sullivan sailed the Clipper through the narrow channel entrance, he felt the flying boat lift up and shudder. Concerned that he had hit a sand bar, he returned to the base. Shortly before dark the Clipper was hauled out of the water; to their astonishment, the ground crew found ten long slices in the hull bottom.

What followed over the next five days appears to have been a cover-up by Pan American. The Alameda *Times-Star* reported on January 6 that the China Clipper had struck a submerged object, while on the same day the San Francisco *Examiner* published a story that the Clipper had hit a floating log. On the 7th, the *Examiner* then wrote that the boat had hit an underwater object, and finally, on the 8th, the *Examiner* once more reported that the damage had been caused by a floating log. Karl Leuder, the Alameda base manager, wrote an entirely different description of the accident in his daily reports. From the very first day, January 5, Pan American knew that the China Clipper had hit a submerged object, not a log.

Between the 5th and the 10th, Leuder's crew combed the lagoon bottom with a U-shaped frame. By the 10th they had discovered several mysterious objects on the bottom of the lagoon. What Leuder found was not reported to the local papers because—like the two Japanese agents caught tampering with the radio direction finder—it would have been impossible to explain. On the bottom of the bay several concrete pedestals with iron rods embedded in the base had been placed so that they stuck up just a few feet below the surface.

The origin of the objects was not discovered, but some at the Alameda base believed that they had been placed there by those who had the most to gain by stopping the Clippers—the Japanese.

Over the past six months an ominous pattern had begun to unfold. First a series of Japanese protests challenged the intent of the trans-Pacific route. Then in November two Japanese were arrested by the FBI while tampering with the

Alameda direction finder and a CNAC passenger liner was forced down by Japanese fighters. And now in January 1936, the mysterious concrete pedestals had torn the bottom out of the China Clipper.

It all pointed to a harrowing future.

14

Amelia Earhart

April 1936-July 1937

*B*Y APRIL THE STORM SEASON had run its course. The vast protective Pacific high pressure system stretching far to sea now settled off California. From this date until October only the morning and afternoon fog intruded past the California coast. A few miles inland scattered fleecy clouds marbled the deep blue sky. Not a drop of rain fell, the temperature remained steady and the barometer never varied more than a few tenths of an inch. The constantly benevolent weather after the worst storm season of the last thirty years now allowed the three Martin Clippers to settle into their regularly scheduled weekly flights to the Far East. The island bases were running smoothly, servicing each flying boat as it came through. The flight crews had begun to learn the idiosyncrasies of the Pacific skies and the Martin Clippers were proving to be the most

150

reliable aircraft in the world, so reliable that in October they would begin carrying passengers. Already, after only six months, flying the Pacific was routine.

Nearly a year had passed since William Miller had colonized Jarvis, Baker, and Howland; and now, Roosevelt, unsure of how to handle their jurisdiction, asked the navy's advice. At first the navy advocated that the atolls be placed under the administration of the Territory of Hawaii but on April 8, 1936, it revised its opinion:

> It is, therefore, recommended that the President be requested to disapprove the proposed Executive Order assigning Jarvis, Baker and Howland Islands to the Department of the Interior and assign these islands to Naval jurisdiction. The reason which may be advanced (confidentially) for this request is that the small U.S. Pacific Islands constitute a natural strategic front from which it would be necessary in time of war to carry on defensive seaplane reconnaissance for the early protection of the Hawaiian Islands. For this reason, it is deemed important that the Navy Department control completely the activities and developments in these potential bases.

For the past twenty-five years Billy Mitchell's warning that the line though the Mandates was vulnerable had haunted the navy. The time was right to string a second Pacific route around Micronesia to the Far East, and as was the case with Wake, the navy too, wanted to control the islands in the South Pacific.

The issue was not as clear to Roosevelt. The transfer of Wake to the navy had generated a great deal of suspicion and even intensified militaristic sentiments in some quarters of Japan. So to avoid aggravating Japan further, Roosevelt, through Executive Order 7368, assigned the islands to the Interior Department. Politically, the transfer was the correct move. Roosevelt knew that the atolls could be reassigned to the navy if the situation changed, but in the meantime commercial aeronautical facilities under the control of the Interior Department would serve the navy equally well. Still, the question remained: How could the government develop these islands without offending Japan?

The answer came from a very unlikely source—Amelia Earhart.

In the fall of 1936, when Earhart announced that she would fly around the world, she planned to fly the Pacific leg of the journey roughly tracing the Clipper route to the Far East. As should have been expected, this route elicited very little excitement from the government, since the flight would not add much to Pacific aviation beyond what Pan American had already done. Through all of November Earhart continued to plan on the mid-Pacific route. But in early December she inexplicably revised her routing and announced that she would fly the South Pacific via Howland Island.

By all appearances it was a foolish and potentially dangerous change of plans. The South Pacific skies, uncharted in 1936, were vast and held unknown dangers. Howland, Earhart's refueling stop, was still a desert island and offered none of the facilities that would have been available to her at any one of the Pan American bases. But now, with this pending new southerly route, Earhart had full and enthusiastic backing from the government.

The pattern of Howland's development was a carbon copy of Pan American's adventure in the mid-Pacific. First, the navy listed Howland as a strategically important atoll as it had Midway, Wake and Guam. Then Earhart, like Trippe, decided to fly the Pacific and finally the government rushed in with moral, physical and financial support to assure the success of the project. From Japan's side of the Pacific the intent of Earhart's flight must have been all too obvious.

The government, which had ignored her original plans in 1936, enthusiastically backed her with $5 million in 1937. Over the next three months the navy, army, coast guard, and Interior Department would invest nearly $5 million and scores of laborers and engineers to build a landing strip and fueling and servicing facilities, and to supply navigational services at Howland Island. It would be worth every penny. Once the strip was constructed and Earhart proved the value of Howland, the navy would have the base it desperately needed south of the equator. The flight across the South Pacific, the route of the nineteenth-century guano miners, would circumvent the Mandates and assure continued communications with Australia, New Zealand, and the British stronghold at Singapore in the coming war.

For all of this planning and money invested in Earhart's flight there were two major flaws. The government, in matters of long-distance navigation, did not have the well-polished expertise of Pan American. Secondly, Earhart's navigator, Fred Noonan, was an alcoholic—a man of dubious talents. Prior to being fired by Pan American, Noonan's abilities had diminished to such an extent that some of the Clipper pilots noticed the courses he plotted were off as much as two hundred miles. For this Pan American dismissed him as untrustworthy. Why did Earhart hire Noonan, then?

At forty-four Noonan had been at sea for thirty years, serving as a navigator on everything from square-riggers to Pan American's Clippers. When he remained sober he was the best; even Ed Musick considered him far and away the finest navigator in the Pacific. He told Earhart that he quit drinking so she may have decided to hire the best. Still, if Noonan began drinking on the flight, he would be an absolute liability, as Pan American had already learned.

Earhart's first attempt to cross the Pacific, in March 1937, failed when she crashed while taking off from Honolulu. Forced to delay the flight until her Lockheed Electra was repaired, she did not begin again until May. This time, due to seasonal weather changes, she flew an easterly course from Oakland across the United States, the Atlantic, and Africa, and by June she landed at Lae, New Guinea, the last stop before the crucial 2,556-mile flight to Howland.

Though Howland was a low-lying atoll, only a mile long and a half-mile wide, with good navigation Earhart should have easily found the island. Noonan had made scores of similar flights for Pan American. The procedure was always the same. Over the open Pacific Noonan's celestial bearings and dead reckoning should have put them within shooting distance of Howland. Then, when they were within the range of the radio direction finders on the coast guard cutter *Itasca* and Howland, Earhart should have been able to find the atoll very quickly. Simple enough, but they had been flying for over a month, Noonan had only had a few hours sleep in the past twenty-four hours, and there were rumors that he had been drinking the night before they left Lae. Compounding these problems, the direction finder on Howland, one of two, was not functioning properly, and Earhart herself was having difficulties.

While the wind was light and the air clear at Howland, Earhart flew through overcast most of the dark morning hours. As the first light of day began to brighten the far horizon, Earhart began to sense the developing trouble. At 6:44 she radioed the longest communication of the flight. There was notable tension in her voice. "Please take bearing on us and report in half hour. I will make noise in microphone. About 100 miles out." Still the message was too short for the *Itasca* to make a bearing. For the next hour the cutter repeatedly tried to contact Earhart but she did not respond.

At 7:42 the sun rose in a blinding glare over Howland and with it Earhart's next message crackled, "KHAQQ calling *Itasca*. We must be on you but cannot see you. But gas is running low. Been unable to reach you by radio. We are flying at altitude 1000 feet." Earhart's voice was shrill.

Indeed, she must have been very close to Howland at this point because the radio signal was as strong as it had been all during the morning and getting stronger. At 7:58 Earhart called again, "KHAQQ calling *Itasca*. We are circling but cannot hear you. Go ahead. . ." For the next fifteen minutes the transmission from Earhart never ran more than 8 seconds and she talked so rapidly the crew on the cutter had great difficulty understanding her. By 8:07 the crew on both Howland and the *Itasca* knew they were in an emergency situation—she was overdue and by mathematical calculation her fuel was nearly exhausted.

At 8:45 Earhart made one last plea to the *Itasca*. "We are on a line position 157 degrees, 337 degrees. Will repeat this message on 6210 kilocycles. Wait, listening on 6210 kilocycles. We are running north and south."

The message was confusing and incomplete. The line position of 157-337 degrees did not give the *Itasca* a specific reference point. At 10:00 the *Itasca* assumed Earhart was down somewhere in the northwest quadrant off Howland and began laying down a thick smoke screen hoping to attract her.

Earhart's loss proved one irrefutable point: Howland was not the right base for South Pacific operations. This disaster taught the navy what Pan Am had long known: only permanent, well-organized facilities operated by skilled technicians on an island larger than Howland could guarantee the safety of trans-oceanic flights. The navy needed a new island. The island, although it was a British possession, would be Canton, the ruse to develop the atoll would be once again Pan American Airways.

Even before the tragic failure of the Earhart flight, the United States, constantly searching for strategic atolls, expressed some interest in the northernmost atoll of the Phoenix Group, Canton Island. In early 1937, the State Department's legal adviser, Ralph Hill, investigated the background of Canton when the *National Geographic* magazine asked the navy for assistance in landing a group of scientists on the atoll to observe a total eclipse of the sun. Among the very few atolls in the Phoenix Group that had not been issued a guano certificate in the nineteenth century, Hill noted that Great Britain had been the last country to visit the island—in 1886. Hill also wrote, to the consternation of the State Department, that Britain had just annexed Canton Island on March 18. Several months later, in August, Samuel Boggs of the State Department's History Section submitted a second report about Canton, confirming the findings of the Legal Department and noting that an American counterclaim to Canton would be flimsy at best.

But the State Department was not prepared to accede to the British claim, regardless of the opinions of the legal or historical sections, and set out to devise a plan to wrest Canton from Britain. Before the project could be set in motion, though, the attention of the diplomatic corps was drawn away from the South Pacific to Asia. Japan was tearing the heart out of China.

China had historically been the route to industrial wealth and political power in the Far East; Japan, a few miles from China across the East China Sea, knew this better than anyone. Recent ferment among Japan's military officers, the pressures of an exploding population, and demand for more raw materials to fuel its factories conspired to make a Japanese invasion of China virtually inevitable. But China was also the keystone of Western power in the Orient. And this conflict was never more evident than in Shanghai.

15

The Shanghai Incident

August 1937-October 1937

IN 1937, CHINA WAS CLEARLY in an emergency situation. Since 1932, there had been sporadic clashes between the Imperial army and Chiang Kai-shek's troops, and earlier in the summer of 1937, serious fighting had finally erupted on the Marco Polo Bridge just ten miles north of Peking. This major confrontation and the conflicts of the past years had forced thousands of refugees out of the war zone south to Shanghai. The newly arrived peasants and the residents of Shanghai felt safe, and well they should have.

Shanghai was an international city and, in a very real sense, separate from the rest of China's problems. Foreign passenger liners made regular trips up the Whangpoo River to Shanghai through the summer of 1937, and in August, the USS *Augusta*, flagship of the American Asiatic Fleet, and the British-built Japanese cruiser *Idumo* were both anchored in the Whangpoo. In the international sections of the city some forty-five thousand Europeans and four thousand Americans led reasonably safe, well-ordered lives. In addition to the foreign civilian population, Shanghai housed a regiment of U.S. Marines, Britain's China Squadron, a thousand French Indo-Chinese troops, and a small band of Italian Fascists. In Shanghai's Hongkew District, a fair number of Japanese bluejackets were also on duty. Around the international kernel lived four million Chinese, making Shanghai the sixth largest city in the world.

In many ways, Shanghai projected the ideal image of a bustling Far Eastern market. Its international flavor and relative political stability caused many to believe that the war would never touch the city. The *North China Herald*, one of Shanghai's English-language newspapers, counted the city as a model for international cooperation in one of its editorials in early August 1937:

> The development of the Sino-Japanese crisis, with all of its attendant uncertainties and anxieties has been reviewed by Shanghai with admirable calm. The steadiness of the market has reflected this composure. No less a tribute should be paid to the Japanese, whose officials and non-officials alike have observed an unruffled courtesy, sturdy common sense and propriety of demeanor. The crisis has undoubtedly aroused great anxiety. Both Chinese and Japanese view the prospect of a breakdown in the efforts to avoid war with real apprehension. Yet, somehow, they have managed to maintain an unaffected placidity. Sino-Japanese friendship must find its place in the sun. In fact, Western controversialists might well take a lesson from this Eastern restraint.

This composure and sense of vitality were the primary moods of the city. But editorials had not created this tenor; instead, it was the people in Shanghai's streets.

The markets had been busy through the summer. Porcelain, carved ivory, Mah-Jongg sets, exotic birds, and fighting crickets were stacked high in shops. Food was lavishly displayed in open-air markets—red varnished ducks and chickens, beef flanks, and fish from the East China Sea. Dentists offered the more affluent Chinese gold teeth and jade fillings. A walk along the Bund, Shanghai's broad riverfront boulevard—past office buildings and restaurants on one side, sampans and stately high-bowed junks threading their way along the Whangpoo on the other—would have confirmed that the city was going about its business as usual. Life could not have been much better for the foreigners living in Shanghai.

Though life was still difficult for millions of peasants, it was better here than in the north where the war raged. In fact, this was one of the better times of the year and many peasants were looking forward to August 8, just days away, when according to superstition, watermelons could be safely eaten. It had been a terribly hot summer, hotter and more humid than usual, and everyone was taking life at a leisurely pace.

Even the correspondents covering the Sino-Japanese War were taking life easy. Ninety percent of all the news from China came through Shanghai and, since travel to the interior was difficult, often dangerous, many of the newsmen simply waited in Shanghai for the news to filter into the hotel bars. On the evening of August 8, one item, at least for a short time, escaped everyone's attention in the international settlement.

At 6:30 it was still light, and in the western outskirts of Shanghai Japanese seaman Yozo Saito drove his officer, Second Lieutenant Isao Oyama, north along Monument Road. Near the Chinese military Hungjao Aerodrome, Chinese guards hailed Saito to stop. He pulled to the side of the road.

Outraged that he had been halted, Oyama climbed out of the car and began arguing with the guards, demanding to know how they could presume to hail an officer of the Imperial navy. Guns were drawn and Oyama was shot through the head. Saito, pulled from the car and beaten, died several hours later.

The news of this incident quickly found its way back to the *Idumo* where it was interpreted as an affront to the Japanese Empire. Admiral K. Hasegawa met with Mayor Yui of Shanghai and demanded that all Chinese troops withdraw from the city. Days of intense negotiations followed with no results.

By the afternoon of August 13, rumors began to circulate among the newsmen in the bars at the Cathay and Palace Hotels that nine thousand Japanese bluejackets had landed at Woosung, just sixteen miles down the Whangpoo. Others said that they heard that thirty thousand Japanese troops were arriving at that very minute at the North Station. But these were only rumors, and the afternoon dissolved into relaxed gossip. It was much too hot outside to make the trip to North Station just to follow up one more rumor. Besides, if the talk were true, they would know soon enough; for now, it was more comfortable to pass the afternoon in the air-cooled lounge at the Cathay Hotel and gaze out on the skittering sampans and the massive hulk of the *Idumo*.

Then, at 4:27, to everyone's horror, the aircraft batteries of the *Idumo* cracked into action. Black splotches of the exploding shells peppered the sky over the Whangpoo. At the same instant, a Chinese fighter strayed off course, accidentally dropping its bombs near the Bund, tearing twenty-foot chunks out of the Nanking Road in front of Pan Am's ticket office.

In the Palace Hotel guests hurled themselves across the lounge to find shelter under tables and chairs. Outside, an oil dump erupted into a spectacular fire; simultaneously, a bomb from a Chinese fighter hit a Japanese aircraft battery. Near the Cathay Hotel, Americans, rushing through a hole in the wall, scrambled for cover. In the French section at the Great World Amusement Park, a single five-hundred-pound bomb killed four hundred panic-stricken Chinese.

In a few days, thirty-seven truck loads of bodies would be hauled from the Amusement Park. Within just hours after the initial fighting broke out, Shanghai looked like a meat locker. Gutters were awash with blood, mangled bodies were draped grotesquely in store fronts and pieces of torn flesh were ground into the pavement by the stampeding crowds. The truth went far beyond the rumors of a few hours earlier.

The war in China had already lasted much longer than the Imperial army had predicted. Frustrated, it attacked Shanghai with a mindless fury. Fully half of the Japanese navy was massed south of Shanghai, pounding the city with its cannons as gunboats ferried troops ashore.

On the morning of the second day, the Bund was packed with thousands trying to escape the burning city. For several hours, the Japanese guns were silent. Then in mid-morning, as the summer heat began to envelop the city, the signal light aboard the *Idumo* winked out a message, just as a Japanese seaplane swooped down and landed near the cruiser. The crowd, sensing something was about to happen, scattered in a screaming, chaotic mass along the Bund. Again, the *Idumo*'s batteries snapped into action.

Over the next few weeks the process repeated itself day after day, and the Imperial army ran amuck in a spree of bloodletting and destruction. Factories were dynamited, Chinese ships were sunk in the Whangpoo, and Shanghai was set ablaze. The war in China had begun in earnest.

In October, flexing its muscles, the Imperial army moved 160 miles northwest, attacking Nanking with such a frenzy that it made the invasion of Shanghai seem tame. Sixteen massive air raids smashed the city. The battle continued through the fall. Hundreds of thousands of Chinese were killed. Finally, even Nazi Germany called for a halt to the slaughter.

These battles were by no means clear victories for Japan. As the Japanese advanced, Chiang Kai-shek withdrew a little deeper, telling the Imperial army more accurately than words ever could that the war would not soon be over.

Though the Imperial army wantonly killed hundreds of thousands in the fall of 1937, China was not entirely innocent in the matter. From the first days of the invasion of Shanghai, Chiang Kai-shek did little to discourage the ferocity of the Japanese attack and, in fact, allowed the incident to expand, hoping that once the West saw the full fury of the Japanese war machine, it would come to his aid. It did not work. The West was not ready for war, certainly not on behalf of Shanghai or Nanking.

The war in China cut deeply into Pan American's Pacific operations. Several of CNAC's aircraft were destroyed by Japanese gun fire, causing Trippe to suspend air service in China temporarily.

On September 9, Trippe met with Stanley Hornbeck in Washington. Explaining that the invasion of Shanghai had ruined any hope that Pan American would make a profit in China for years, Trippe also confided that CNAC had been commandeered by Chiang Kai-shek and was being used by the military during the present crisis. Trippe knew that CNAC under military control would damage the image of the trans-Pacific line, as well as make it difficult to convince business-men to fly to or in China. "The company has kept all of this out of the newspapers and we should keep it confidential for the time being," he said. Hornbeck understood Trippe's dilemma.

Just as Trippe was leaving, he mentioned one more point

that had bothered him for several days. Trippe told Hornbeck that Mr. Kadono, head of the Japanese economic mission in the United States, had asked him about using one of Pan Am's Pacific bases as a Japanese air terminal. Trippe said Kadono was most interested in Hawaii and Guam but confessed he did not know what to tell Kadono and wondered what Hornbeck made of it. Hornbeck thought for a moment and told Trippe point-blank, "It's time that American business begin discouraging Japanese advances such as this."

16

Sabotage

October 1937-July 1938

T HE PASSIONS OF AUGUST had cooled by October.
Over the past two and a half months the British
had steadfastly refused to compromise their claim to Canton
Island—to the dismay of the State Department. On October
21, 1937, Assistant Secretary of State R. Walton Moore,
hoping to resolve the matter, dictated a letter to Cordell Hull
outlining the British position:

> The Chargé said that his government is not disputing our
> ownership of Howland, Jarvis and Baker, but is declining
> to admit that there is any doubt about the British
> ownership of Canton. . . . I at once informed the President
> of all this, leaving it to him to determine whether he will
> discuss the matter with Admiral Leahy and me before he
> goes to Hyde Park tomorrow. . . .

Anxious to settle the Canton issue, Roosevelt called Moore and Leahy to the White House later the same afternoon. They talked for only a few minutes before Roosevelt declared that he did not think that they could really make a final decision without first speaking to Sir Ronald Lindsay, the British ambassador. Lindsay, now in London, would not return to Washington for several more weeks, so they mutually agreed to postpone any further action until the ambassador's return.

Curiously, at the same time as the White House meeting, Juan Trippe was independently setting a plan in motion that would be the prime force to help take Canton from Britain. For nearly two years Trippe had delayed opening the South Pacific route, because of equipment shortages, but now, on October 21, he decided to recall the Hong Kong Clipper, an S-42, to Honolulu to begin a series of survey flights to Auckland.

By early December the Hong Kong Clipper had been refitted with long-distance fuel tanks and renamed the Samoan Clipper. Ed Musick had not heard about the new route, but when he returned home from his first vacation in years, he received orders to take command of the Samoan Clipper.

Musick had been flying over 130 hours a month for over two years, nearly a third more than the domestic airline pilots were flying. The long, grueling trans-Pacific flights were beginning to age Musick beyond his forty-three years. Though everyone on the Pacific line faced the long hours, Musick also blazed all of the new routes and training all the crews. It was becoming too much for Cleo to overlook.

On the evening before Musick left, December 12, he and Cleo talked in their eighth-floor apartment. Outside, the lights of Sausalito sparkled from the far shore, on the bay, red and green running lights marked the path of a freighter as it plowed under the Golden Gate. They reminisced about a picnic they took during a recent spate of good weather. Their conversation was almost melancholy; Musick had spent half of their recent life away and now he told Cleo that he would be in New Zealand for Christmas. Cleo, really wanting to talk about the future and not the past, asked him to cut down the number of flights or maybe take an office job. Musick knew that he pressed his luck on each of the exploratory flights, but he just shrugged and tried to console Cleo.

The first survey flight through Kingman Reef and Samoa came off without a hitch and Musick thought he would be back in San Francisco by January 20, 1938. The second flight, carrying assorted light freight—clothing, automotive parts, and newsreels of the war in China—went as well as the first. But after Musick landed at Pago Pago on January 11, everything seemed to go wrong.

Pago Pago harbor, surrounded by precipitous 1,500-foot mountain walls, was the most inspiring body of water in all of Polynesia. The still bay, the lush tropical foliage, and the gentle breezes engendered an idyllic charm. But it was not a good seaplane port. Though the take-off into the prevailing wind through the channel entrance was a clear shot, the landing at Pago Pago was the most difficult final approach Musick had ever encountered. The landing into the harbor required that the Clipper make a steep approach from the north, skimming over the mountaintops, and then, at the last moment, dive for the harbor. Not only did the landing call for inordinate pilot skill but the flying boat itself had to perform to the limits of its capabilities to make the tricky maneuver.

At the graying dawn on January 12, Musick, fatigued by the last three weeks in the South Pacific, and his six-man crew climbed aboard the Samoan Clipper. Several dozen curious Samoans in their outrigger canoes delayed the take-off a few minutes but once the path was cleared Musick throttled the engines to full power. With the speed of the Clipper climbing steadily—60, 70, 80—Musick pumped on the control yoke to break the suction of the water on the ship's hull. Finally, after thirty seconds, the Clipper responded to Musick's command, lifting its nose toward the open Pacific.

It was truly a magnificent day. The green island slipped away and the brilliant tropical morning spread out before Musick like a diorama. Barely out of the harbor, Musick banked the Clipper into a south by west heading and settled back for the day-long flight. But no sooner had the exhilaration of the take-off subsided than Flight Engineer J. W. Stickrod called up to the bridge that engine number four had developed an oil leak. Musick told Stickrod to shut the engine down. It was 6:08.

Musick thought ahead. They would have to return to Pago Pago, dump fuel to lighten the ship for the landing, make a northern approach over the mountains, keep engine r.p.m. high. There was no alarm, only concern; Musick had made scores of difficult landings. After all, it was only an oil leak, it was not an emergency.

At 6:45 Musick flew over Pago Pago harbor, sizing up the approach once more, and then shouted over to his co-pilot, C. G. Sellers, that he was going to burn off some fuel before they landed. He banked the Clipper toward British Apia, just 75 miles to the west. By 8:00 Musick was heading back for Pago Pago.

Flying at ten thousand feet and some twenty miles out of the harbor, Musick went into his landing configuration and Stickrod opened the dump valves. Located on the underside of each wing, the dump valves had been designed to lighten the aircraft for emergency landings. Musick considered them a safety device. From each valve long plumes of gasoline sprayed into the air as Musick lowered the wing flaps.

At the same moment the Clipper nosed down, something

began to occur that no one in the Clipper noticed. The lowered wing flaps had created giant whirlwinds; they raced around the Clipper, sucking the vaporized gasoline back around the ship's hull. Musick, preoccupied with the landing, ran through the approach into the harbor once more. Then, in an instant that was never realized, the torching exhaust flames from the engines exploded the vaporized fuel.

At the moment of the blast Radio Officer T. Findley was talking to Pago Pago. After the signal abruptly stopped, a swarm of conflicting reports circulated through the base. Some said the Clipper probably had landed in Apia. Others believed that Musick had landed outside the bay and the high mountains blocked the radio signals. For the time being no one believed the two Samoan boys who said they saw the flying boat explode.

On the following day the U.S.S. *Avocet*, searching along the west coast of the island near Cape Taputapu, radioed to Pago Pago: "Heavy oil slick. Have motor launch recovering parts of wrecked plane. Identification satisfactory." For most of the day the *Avocet* fished bits of the wreckage from the water. Nothing larger than six square inches was found—scraps of trousers, part of Radio Officer Findley's perforated coat, a section of the chart board, pages from the engineer's log, a lapel with a Pan American emblem on it. Days later the oil slick and all the thousands of pieces that represented the shredded Clipper dispersed. By the time the search was completed, it was evening in San Francisco. Calling from Alameda, Clarence Young told Cleo that they had found the wreckage of the Clipper. All were lost. Ed had been killed.

The loss of a first-line crew, a flying boat, and Musick forced Trippe to close the South Pacific line. The decision hit the navy very hard. In approving Pan American's application for additional space at Pearl Harbor for the extra flying boats that would have been used on the flights to New Zealand, the Bureau of Aeronautics wrote:

> ... In view of the obvious benefits derived by the Navy Department from commercial aircraft operations of this nature where aircraft operating information and facilities will be pioneered in important strategic areas, it is considered that some inconvenience resulting from the use of Navy servicing facilities involved in this case is acceptable. ...

But like the Earhart tragedy, the loss of the Samoan Clipper revealed the navy's underlying vulnerability in the South Pacific. As recently as six months ago, the navy was certain that Howland, Kingman Reef, and Samoa would become first-class air bases. Now all of that was lost. Kingman, nothing more than a coral reef bobbing in the middle of the Pacific, was not large enough to service more than one flying boat at a time, much less support a land runway. Now the steep cliffs surrounding Pago Pago proved that Samoa could handle seaplane operations only under the most ideal circumstances. In the spring of 1938, out of all the atolls the United States claimed, not one could handle sophisticated air operations.

The navy did not suffer this discontent alone. Nearly a year had passed since Britain claimed Canton and the State Department knew, as more time passed, that it would be more difficult, maybe impossible, to sustain an American counter-claim for the atoll. Not only was time running out but now the United States needed Canton. Barely two weeks had passed since the accident at Samoa when R. Walton Moore wrote Roosevelt suggesting two courses that he believed would secure Canton for American interests. The first called for pressure.

Moore thought that Roosevelt might meet with Ambassador Lindsay and try to persuade him of the legitimacy of the

American claim, though he conceded that this would probably fail. Since Lindsay had used such talks in the past to postpone making a decision, Moore favored a second, more aggressive plan, which also received the backing of the Navy and Interior Departments. Moore continued:

. . . Transfer by Executive Order to the administration of the Interior Department (a) the islands of the Phoenix Group, to which we make claim, particularly Canton, Enderbury, Phoenix, and McKean Islands, or (b) a more extensive list covering all of the islands in mid-Pacific to which we make claim, even though we might abandon many such claims at a later date by virtue of an agreement with the British . . .

At the same time, you might authorize the dispatch of the revenue cutter *Itasca* with settlers and equipment for Canton . . .

We would then be in the situation of having, on some of the islands, both American and British settlers side by side—while awaiting a diplomatic settlement of the issue . . . .

On January 24, Legal Adviser Ralph Hill wrote the Legal Department's opinion of Moore's plan:

. . . Up till the British Order in Council of March, 1937, no action had been taken by the British with respect to Canton, so far as our records show, which would have precluded the United States from asserting a claim to that island. In view, however, of the Order in Council and of the fact that Canton has never appertained to the United States, it is doubted that we have any legal claim to the island. There is a probability that the island was for a long time occupied by an American guano company. However, there does not appear to have been any occupation of the island by Americans for the last sixty years or more. . . .

It is not believed that there is any existing specific authority of law under which the President could act in placing these islands under the Department of Interior for administrative purposes. . . .

As though the Samoan Clipper disaster and the thorniness of the Canton negotiations were not enough to dismay Trippe, Pan American at the same time was faced with what appeared to be another round of Japanese sabotage aimed at closing down the trans-Pacific line. In light of the past sabotage attempts, Pan American moved with notable caution.

Late in the afternoon of January 29, Robert Thach, Pan Am's vice president and trouble shooter in Washington, met privately with E. A. Tarn, special FBI agent. A preliminary investigation conducted by Pan Am into the loss of the Samoan Clipper, Thach said, had revealed that the flying boat was destroyed not by a gasoline explosion but by a bomb which had been planted in the boat's hull. A second suspicious incident occurred just ten days later when the China Clipper enroute to Honolulu developed trouble in its fuel lines which forced the ship back to California. Two days after this, Thach continued, the same problem appeared again in the China Clipper between Honolulu and Midway. Thach told Tarn that on both occasions base mechanics discovered small corks in the seawing fuel tanks which had plugged the feeder lines and stopped the flow of fuel to two of the engines. Thach said that he and other executives in New York were certain that both of these incidents were the result of sabotage.

Tarn listened intently and agreed to take these incidents under advisement. As soon as Thach left, Tarn forwarded a memorandum of the conversation to J. Edgar Hoover, suggesting that the Bureau take on the investigation. Hoover emphatically agreed and scribbled across the bottom of Tarn's memo, "Proceed with it but it must be handled confidentially if we are to get results."

Two days later after a follow-up meeting with Thach, Tarn wrote a detailed four-page report to Hoover that in part explained the source of Pan American's anxiety. Prefacing his report with background information from Thach which explained that Pan American had experienced three previous incidents of sabotage* in the Pacific division, Tarn wrote that it appeared that Japan had sanctioned these incidents as well:

"... Mr. Thach stated that the Japanese government
has been hostile towards the trans-Pacific line flights at all
times, this hostility being predicated upon several
elements, primarily the fact that the Americans had taken
the initiative in pioneering the flights across the Pacific,
therefore discrediting the Japanese enterprises. Further
hostility is based upon the fact that the termination of the
route is in China rather than in Japan. Further hostility
arose from the fact that in order to secure the consent of the
Chinese government for the use of Shanghai as an Eastern
Terminal of the line, the Pan American Corporation had
formed a partnership with the Chinese government. . . ."

Tarn continued:

"... The cork disks are not part of the supplies or

* The FBI report is not specific but Thach was probably referring to the November 1935 radio direction finder incident and the January 1936 discovery of the sunken concrete pedestals. The third reference has not been uncovered by the author.

equipment maintained by the Pan American lines. Mr.
Thach stated that the few people who know about
these incidents are virtually frantic over the fact that
sabotage is again being attempted upon their ships.
They can attribute no motive to any person other than
the Japanese jealousy of the operation of their
lines. . . ."

Thach's analysis was only partially correct. Certainly
Japan had been openly hostile to Pan American and should
have been the prime suspect but not for the chauvinistic
reasons Thach suggested. Nor could the hostility have been
based upon Japanese jealousy of Pan Am terminating in
China instead of Japan because Japanese officials had denied
Pan American landing rights in Japan several times over the
last few years. Thach completely miscalculated the source of
Japan's fear. What concerned Japan far above anything else
was simply the strategic advantage the trans-Pacific line gave
the American navy.

With seven men killed in the Samoan Clipper, the apparent
sabotage of the China Clipper and the potential international
repercussions in this case, the FBI opened the investigation
cautiously. Tarn told Thach that because of the international
sensitivity of this matter that absolutely no one except
key personnel at Pan American should be informed about the
investigation. They had decided, Tarn said, to place an undercover
agent at the Alameda base who would work as a
mechanic's helper.

While the investigation at Alameda continued, Trippe
was also busy following the Canton Island developments at the
State Department. On February 11, certain that Pan Am
would gain from an American claim to Canton, Trippe wrote
Cordell Hull asking for permission to build aeronautical facilities
on the atoll.

Trippe pressed for an immediate reply and just five days after his letter to Hull he met with Pierrepont Moffat, head of the State Department's Division of European Affairs. Trippe pushed for an answer: "How long will it take to get an answer—a month, six weeks?" Moffat told Trippe they were not yet in a position to answer but were very happy to have received his letter.

If possible, Roosevelt was even more anxious to claim Canton than Trippe, though he had entirely different reasons. Seeing that Europe was on a course toward war, Roosevelt was certain that Britain would defend the homeland first, leaving its Pacific colonies vulnerable to Japanese occupation. He did not want to take the chance that Canton, lying on the southern flank of Hawaii within the distance of long-range bombers, would become one more Japanese base pointed at Pearl Harbor.

On the same afternoon that Trippe spoke to Moffat, Roosevelt called Moore, Dr. Gruening, head of the Interior Department's Division of Territorial Affairs, and Moffat to the White House so that he could dictate how they would solve the question of Canton's sovereignty. Moffat typed up a memorandum of the conversation and marked it Secret:

The President said that he had sent for us in order to discuss ways and means of getting the use of a number of islands in the Pacific. It was clear to him that the approach we had made last summer through Sir Ronald Lindsay was not producing any results. He thought that the time had come when we must bring Ambassador Kennedy into the picture. He had accordingly discussed the matter with Mr. Kennedy the night before last and had instructed him to take up very shortly after his arrival in London the whole subject with Mr.

Neville Chamberlain personally. He was to point out that there were in the Pacific several hundreds, if not thousands, of islands; that both Britain and the United States had conflicting claims to many of these islands; that we saw nothing to be gained by entering into legalistic discussions as to the sovereignty of individual islands; that this would be a long drawn out process and possibly acrimonious; that both Great Britain and the United States had a common interest in all of these islands, namely to keep a third party out of the area, namely Japan. . . .

Roosevelt was in no mood to be trifled with on this issue. He wanted the British to compromise. If they did not, he told his advisers, Kennedy had instructions on what to say:

With this background Mr. Kennedy was to inform Mr. Neville Chamberlain that unless we perceived a different attitude toward our perfectly reasonable suggestion for settlement of the status of the islands under dispute, the President would sign an Executive Order placing under the jurisdiction of the United States Interior Department all islands not permanently occupied in the areas generally situated between Samoa and Hawaii and he would furthermore send settlers in quantities to such unoccupied islands. . . .

Since the British had already established a small settlement on Canton in what Roosevelt considered a breach of a previous agreement, he instructed Gruening to send American settlers aboard the *Itasca* on its February 25 voyage to the South Pacific and land them on Canton. Roosevelt noted the *Itasca*'s arrival at Canton would coincide with Kennedy's meeting with Chamberlain, thereby convincing the British of the seriousness of his intentions.

As he had warned, Roosevelt did not hesitate. On March 3, he signed an Executive Order placing Canton under American sovereignty. Four days later American colonists from the *Itasca* landed on the atoll.

Less than a week after Roosevelt signed the Executive Order, Trippe was on the telephone asking Moffat if the State Department would object if he applied to the Interior Department for use of the atoll. Moffat thought that it was still too early to go that far but agreed that he could talk to the Interior Department on an informal basis. Trippe hung up and called the Interior Department for an appointment. The next day, March 8, Trippe was in Dr. Gruening's office in Washington. Canton was vital to Pan American's plans in the South Pacific and Trippe, disregarding Moffat's caution, actually asked for permission to build an air base on the atoll. Gruening said that would be a matter for consideration by the secretary of the interior.

The following day, when Gruening informed Moffat that Trippe had actually asked for rights through Canton, Moffat became angry, but Gruening asked him, "Wouldn't it ease our position to let Pan American use Canton without delay?"

It would indeed. On April 1, while formal Canton negotiations were still in progress with the British, the Interior Department released a press announcement saying that landing rights had been granted to Pan Am at Canton Island. Though the sovereignty of Canton was still under dispute, once Pan Am was given landing rights, the atoll essentially became an American possession.

Trippe was still over a year away from inaugurating the line but the navy's problem in the South Pacific had been solved and the timing was right. A Pacific war was closer than ever.

Over the past few weeks the Alameda FBI investigation

had produced disarmingly little information. The undercover agent had gained the confidence of the ground crew and at work engaged them in casual conversations about the Samoan and China Clipper's incidents. When this failed to produce any information, he followed the crew to Martin's Bar near the Alameda base, where over a few beers he pursued the covert investigation. This tactic failed as well.

In the early spring, at the suggestion of Colonel Clarence Young, the Director of the Pacific Division, the investigation assumed a broader scope. Young conceded that Japan could be behind the sabotage but he also felt that the incidents may have been inspired by communist-backed labor groups. Since the investigation had hit a dry hole the FBI agreed to concentrate on the communist angle. But still the Bureau found nothing.

Late in the spring the Oakland FBI admitted that they were stymied and suggested that they end the undercover work and open up the investigation. Young disagreed. He was certain if this happened, the matter would leak to the press and discredit Pan Am. The qualms Young expressed to the FBI precisely identified why Pan American did not release information about this and the previous cases of sabotage in the 1930s. The Oakland FBI agent quoted Young in his report to Washington: ". . . It is conceivable that the operating permit of the company would be withdrawn, the general public would become aware of what has occurred and it might take the company years to overcome the adverse publicity. . . ."

In spite of Young's strenuous objections the FBI did begin to quietly confront several of Pan American's most suspicious employees openly but still nothing, not detailed questioning, not scientific analysis of the Clippers, not even the extended covert observations, had discovered anything which pointed to Japanese or communist-backed sabotage.

After a five-month exhaustive investigation the FBI closed the case when it determined that one mechanic as a matter of personal habit used corks to prevent foreign debris from falling in the tanks while they were cleaned. The corks found in the China Clipper's seawings had simply been misplaced. Shortly afterwards, Pan American's board of inquiry concluded that the Samoan Clipper had indeed immolated itself. On the approach to Pago Pago one dump valve stuck and released too much fuel which in turn was ignited by the engine's exhaust flames.

Though Japan had not tampered with the Samoan and China Clippers the five-month investigation and the concern about the possibility of sabotage was well founded. The past years proved that anything could happen.

Now, the Hawaii Clipper was en route to Macao, and in defiance of the Imperial army, Wah Sun Choy was carrying $3 million to Chungking.

17

Guam:
The Final Hours

July 29, 1938

THE PAN AMERICAN HOTEL AT SUMAY, GUAM.
Wah Sun Choy woke from a deep sleep. His night
clothes were damp. He had not had a nightmare, nor did he
feel particularly upset; but when he perspired this way he
knew that something was disturbing him.

It was just after 4:00 A.M.; the sun would not rise for
another two hours. Apart from the hotel manager walking
down the hall, knocking on each door and calling the passengers to breakfast, there was not another sound. This silence
and the blackness were the two most identifiable qualities of
the morning.

Though this was the fourth day of waking at 4:00 A.M.,
Choy had not found it any easier to get out of bed than it had
been on the first morning in Honolulu. Suddenly something
occurred to him which he thought may have caused him

to perspire so heavily: he was on the edge of the Orient.

China was less than two days away; on the third day, he thought, he would be in Chungking. The previous days at Honolulu, Midway, Wake had been fun, carefree. There had been something of a light, tropical feeling about each of these islands, but Guam was different. It seemed oppressive. The wind ruffled a palm frond against the window; Choy turned quickly to see what had made the noise.

Choy knew he was apprehensive about today's flight because everything after today would be different. Meier and McKinley would temporarily terminate their trip in Manila while the other four would go on to China. French would catch the first flight out of Macao for Canton, and Wyman—well, Choy was not sure where Wyman was off to but he assumed Indo-China or India. Kennedy would stay at the Tai Shan base in Macao while he worked on some scheduling problems. Choy thought he would leave for Chungking as soon as possible and visit his mother and sister on his return trip.

So after five days together this would be the last flight they would make as a group. This saddened Choy. He thought the group had gotten along together very well. They had their own jokes and some things in common; it seemed a shame that they would never see one another again. This bittersweet realization forced him to recall the morning he overlooked Waikiki from his room at the Royal Hawaiian. That was the best moment of the trip, he thought.

In the dining room, at the far end of the hotel, the tables had been set last night for breakfast. Neatly placed at each setting, the coffee cups had been turned upside down and rolls and fruit had been placed in the center of the tables for those who preferred a light breakfast. The Hawaii Clipper's crew had already eaten and had left to prepare for the flight when the passengers wandered in. Choy was the last to arrive. He

entered with a broad, almost affected smile and greeted everyone by name like the restaurant owner that he was.

While the passengers ate, Terletsky and Walker re-
viewed the day's weather forecast. Occasionally, a typhoon or
the threat of one delayed some late summer flights out of
Guam a day or two but today the forecast predicted no such
problem. The flight to Manila was broken into three weather
zones and the weather had been predicted to be remarkably
uniform in each zone. As Terletsky read the report he mum-
bled half aloud those sections that he wanted Walker to pick
up: "Scattered showers, chance of a thunderstorm near the
Philippine coast. Visibility good, cloud tops at eight to ten
thousand feet. Eighty degrees Sumay, eighty-one Manila.
Barometer steady, one tenth of an inch lower at Manila." He
put the report down, "Looks like a good day."

Yesterday afternoon, shortly after the Hawaii Clipper
landed, the ground crew had hauled the ship out of the harbor
and rolled it into an old Marine hangar. Open to the sea, Apra
harbor sometimes becomes very rough and since beaching
facilities were available, the Clippers were pulled ashore for
the night. Not only did this protect the flying boats; it also
made the overnight servicing a much simpler procedure than
at Midway and Wake. Through the afternoon and into the
early evening, while Chamorros cleaned the interior of the
Clipper, two base mechanics performed the prescribed overnight service. The Hawaii Clipper, in excellent condition, had
completed thirty-five trips to the Far East, logging 4,700
flawless hours. Other than checking lubrication and making a
few fine adjustments, there was little for the mechanics to do.
Cox had not listed any important mechanical items that
needed repair on the flight from Wake. Actually, it would
have been highly irregular had the Hawaii Clipper required
major work.

Each of the Martins was well cared for on a daily basis,

and after one returned to Alameda it was virtually torn apart and rebuilt—to check for structural and mechanical deficiencies. When the Hawaii Clipper left Alameda on July 23, in accordance with company policy two of its four engines and propellers were new and the other two had been in operation only 140 hours.

About the same time the mechanics finished, the two Japanese officers from Saipan left the fisherman's cabin near Point Pagat for the fifteen-mile trek across the island. They had made the hike to Sumay so many times before they had little concern about being discovered.

They were certain that the Clipper had two main storage areas and that they would be able to hide in the rear compartment. They felt that the smaller of the two compartments, located under the bridge, was too small and too close to the ship's activity to be really safe. The rear compartment, extending from the boarding steps to the tail, represented nearly a fifth of the Clipper's total length. They hoped this would be an ideal place to conceal themselves. There was nothing for them to be concerned about; the floor plan was accurate and the hangar, which simplified the mechanical check, was also perfect cover for them when they slipped aboard the Clipper.

At 5:30 A.M., after a short ride from the hotel, a launch carried the six passengers out to the Clipper in the harbor. Boarding the ship through the front side hatch, as the Clipper rocked with the swells, required athletic dexterity. Almost directly above their heads the whirling propellers stirred the harbor, and as the launch dipped into the trough of a wave the Clipper heaved up. Actually, boarding the Clipper this way was more exhilarating than dangerous, but even so, just as French jumped from the launch only a quick hand from Parker saved him from falling into the water.

Choy, like the others, camped in the same seat he had sat

in on each of the preceding days. Buckling himself in, he looked past the twinkling running light at the tip of the wing, as the launch raced back and forth searching for stray debris. On the bridge, also watching the boat, Terletsky held the Clipper into the wind. A few minutes after 6:00, as the rising sun cut a silhouette of the far shore against the sky, the launch fired a Very pistol. A star shell burst over the harbor, showering green sparks, signalling an OK to Terletsky. He pushed the power button. The engines growled, straining at the mounts. The propellers chewed the air, and, with the same suddenness that occurred every morning, the Clipper plowed into the seas. With the engines pounding out their regular beat through the ship's hull, the pace quickened. For nearly thirty seconds the boat followed the profile of the swells, rising and falling on them like a surfboard. In the last seconds before take-off, the Clipper smacked each wave as it passed, shooting a glorious spume of water high into the air. At 6:08 the Clipper skimmed across the last wave.

Because of a slight tropical depression near the Philippines, Terletsky, following a procedure Musick had instituted for safety reasons, set a course slightly south of the usual route to Manila to avoid the thunderstorm. Through the morning the weather conformed to the Pan Am prediction. From his red leather seat, Terletsky scanned the clouded sky, occasionally looking below to see if he could spot a passing steamer. Walker sat in the right seat and McCarty tapped out half-hour weather and position reports to KMGB at Guam, KZDY at Panay in the central Philippines, and to KXBQ in Manila. It was a dreary chore; except for their position, one message read like the other: moderately rough head winds, scattered showers, speed 105 knots, 10,000 feet.

In the lounge, Wyman thumbed through what were now week-old magazines. In *Time* he studied an article about the war and a map showing that Japan now occupied nearly a quarter of China. A few pages back he read a piece about two scientists who had spent thirty-two days in the Mammoth Caves to discover if man truly lived on a twenty-four-hour cycle. Then it dawned upon him that he had read that article a few days earlier. He tossed the magazine on the center table.

Meier and McKinley were engaged in an animated conversation while Meier assembled his air hook. Since smoking was not allowed, Choy took out a cigar and slowly slipped it under his nose, inhaling the aroma. He had done this several times through the morning and French, sitting next to him, became noticeably irritable every time Choy did this. It only reminded French that it would be hours before he could smoke his second cigarette of the day. Shortly before lunch Choy fumbled through some scraps of paper on which he had written several poems over the past few days. After reading one, he looked up to the ceiling, closed his eyes, and tried to memorize it. Then he looked down and quietly recited it to himself. Kennedy leaned over. "Very nice, Watson."

The Clipper suddenly hit a rain squall that shook the boat hard. The jolt grabbed everyone's attention but in a few minutes the sky cleared revealing a rainbow arching between two clouds in the distance.

At noon McCarty signaled the Hawaii Clipper's call letters, KHAZB, then tapped out his report:

Flying in rough air, 9,100 feet. Temperature 13 degrees centigrade. Wind 19 knots per hour from 247 degrees. Position latitude 12 degrees 27 minutes north. Longitude 130 degrees 40 minutes east. Dead reckoning. Ground speed made good 112 knots. Desired track 282 degrees. Rain. During past hour cloud conditions have varied. 10/10ths of sky covered by cumulus clouds whose tips were 9,200 feet. 5/10ths of hour on instruments. Last direction finder bearing from Manila 101 degrees true.

While McCarty beat out the noon report, Parker passed out the luncheon menu: appetizers, consomme, creamed tuna on toast, peas, fruit cocktail. Jokingly, French called to Parker, "What's this? No salad?" Before Parker had a chance to respond Choy interrupted, "You don't ask for nothing, you don't get nothing." Everyone chuckled. Wyman spoke up. "Leave Parker alone and let him bring out lunch."

Just as Parker turned to the galley he looked back to the door leading to the rear sleeping compartments. "What is this?" As though drawn by a magnet everyone in the lounge fixed his eyes on the door. Standing one behind the other, two small Japanese ordered Parker to sit down. When Parker hesitated, one spoke louder and pointed his revolver at him.

As Parker moved into the lounge, the second officer rushed forward and disappeared into the galley. The remaining Japanese stayed in the door. French was the first to speak. "What is this? What are you doing?"

The Japanese waved the gun toward French. "No questions."

Now at 12:11, Panay, the closest base to the Hawaii Clipper, acknowledged McCarty's report and requested permission to transmit the noon weather sequence. McCarty signaled, "Stand by for one minute before sending as I am having trouble with rain static." McCarty jerked around as a hand pulled the telegraph key out of the radio. "What the hell?" Before he finished the question he saw an Oriental standing between him and Terletsky. Waving his pistol back and forth, the Japanese ordered him to go below and get a heading for Koror Island.

Lying less than four hundred miles to the southwest, Koror had served as the main base for Japanese interests in the Palaus since the Japanese occupation of Micronesia. Since Koror was removed from the main group of Micronesian atolls, the United States had almost no knowledge of the atoll. The only information Washington had about the atoll in 1938 came through a report from the Office of Naval Intelligence to Stanley Hornbeck speculating that the Imperial navy had recently built a secret seaplane base there. Other than that the State Department knew nothing about Koror.

Even before McCarty brought up the new heading, Panay, at 12:12, was back on the air requesting to signal the weather report. But nothing but static could be heard on the carrier waves. For the first 45 minutes there was little concern: losing contact was not unknown. But near 1:00 Panay began to worry—McCarty should have repaired any damage to the radio by this time or switched to one of the two backup units. By 1:30 Alameda decided something had gone wrong and put the Pacific bases on emergency standby. Indeed, something had gone wrong—though Alameda could never have guessed that the Hawaii Clipper had been hijacked and was at that moment on course for Koror.

Not long after the takeover the initial shock subsided. Everything returned to normal. An occasional rain squall still shook the Clipper as it passed through a cloud, Parker had been permitted to serve coffee, and now French had regained his composure and demanded to know what this was all about. The officer refused to answer.

What was happening was something French could not have even imagined. Well over a week earlier, when the Imperial navy was certain that Wah Sun Choy would be aboard the Hawaii Clipper, it instituted this project to stop the delivery of the $3 million he was carrying to Chiang Kai-shek. The plotters were willing to do anything— steal the Clipper, kill the passengers and crew—to impede the Nationalist war effort. But there was a bonus in the plan. Unsure of Kawanishi's aircraft design, the Imperial navy combined purposes. What better way, it was reasoned, to assure Japan of a superior flying boat than by modeling the Emily after the finest seaplane in the world?

All of this was too fantastic for anyone aboard the Clipper to have dreamt—how could anyone have known the desperation of the Japanese military to defeat China, or its need for a modern long-distance flying boat? Still, there must have been a horrifying moment when the passengers and crew realized that there was no turning back, that this deed was irrevocable.

Near 5:00 P.M., not too long before the Hawaii Clipper should have landed at Manila, Koror appeared on the horizon. Choy glanced out the window. The scene looked just as it had on each previous day. It seemed odd. The water sparkled as it always had and just before they landed Parker reminded them to fasten their seat belts.

By 10:00 P.M., Pan American was sure that the Clipper's fuel had been exhausted and that the ship was down. Within two hours the navy organized one of the largest searches in its history. Fifteen vessels, six army long-distance bombers, and two small amphibians were combing the seas between Manila and Guam. Over the next week the ships and aircraft methodically searched—first around the Clipper's last reported position and then spreading out. Some, in the event the flying boat had continued past its noon location, covered the sea, the bays, and the land on the northwest course to Manila. Others backtracked the Hawaii Clipper's course, considering that Terletsky might have decided to return to Guam. After the first full day, canvassing thousands of square miles, nothing was found.

Throughout the course of the search, the best hope lay in the army transport *Meigs*, which was sailing just seventy miles from the Clipper's noon position. Immediately after receiving word from Manila, the *Meigs* began crisscrossing the sea. Like the others, it found nothing on the first day. On the second day the seas remained calm and the skies clear, and in the twenty-ninth hour of the search the *Meigs* spotted a 1,500-foot circle of oil rolling with the sea—only twenty-eight miles from McCarty's noon report. It seemed certain that the slick marked the point where the Clipper crashed into the sea. As night approached the *Meigs* launch scooped several samples of the oil for later chemical analysis.

The *Meigs* did not find anything more. In the ensuing days, the navy expanded the search in an ever-expanding arc. Again and again the bays and shore areas of Samar, Panay, and Luzon were searched—the navy even went as far south as Mindanao—but still nothing more than the slick was discovered. On August 5, after one week, the hunt was abandoned.

As far as the world was concerned, the Hawaii Clipper, a twenty-six-ton flying boat—and the fifteen men aboard— were simply lost at sea.

Epilogue

*E*VEN TODAY ALL OF THE FACTS ABOUT THE Hawaii Clipper's disappearance are not available and there is some mystery why this is so. Still, there is a great deal known about the Clipper's last flight.

On July 31, 1938, William Miller was appointed to the board of inquiry that investigated the Clipper's loss. Upon his appointment Miller said that sabotage would be among his prime concerns in the investigation but strangely nothing about it appears in the official Hawaii Clipper accident report. What is most baffling about this loss is the limited information available when there is so much detail on lesser incidents of suspected and/or real sabotage. So, did this really happen? Could Japanese naval officers really have hijacked the Hawaii Clipper? Yes.

To an extent the flight of the Hawaii Clipper is a composite of all the other previous Clipper flights to China. Also, since all aboard Flight 229 were lost, some conjecture must fill in areas where specific facts are lacking. In general, though, most of the events surrounding Flight 229 are an accurate reflection of what happened. One flight to Hong Kong was pretty much like all of the others and there is no reason to believe that the sights, sounds, and conversations did not actually transpire; most of what appears in these pages about the Hawaii Clipper is far more truth than fiction. The backgrounds of the passengers and crew, the purposes of the flight for Choy, Wyman, and the others are a matter of record.

But some things are harder to nail down.

For instance, the fact that Wah Sun Choy was carrying a substantial amount of money to Chungking is well documented—even today, restaurateurs in Jersey City's Chinatown still recall the story about Choy going to China in 1938. What is impossible to pinpoint, though, is the exact amount of money Choy carried. At the end of 1938, the Chinese War Relief Committee reported that it had raised $6 million over the previous eighteen months. This is a matter of record so it does not seem unreasonable to assume that Choy, as chairman of the relief committee, carried at the very least $1 million and very likely $2 to $3 million, perhaps more.

The mechanical condition of the Hawaii Clipper, times of take-off, the weather, the general mood of the crew, and the unfolding drama of the Hawaii Clipper's last flight from the time it departed Alameda to McCarty's 12:11 radio communication are reported in several documents and firsthand accounts. The only unknown factor about this flight is what happened during the minute between McCarty's last signal and Panay's attempt to raise the Clipper again. It is universally agreed that whatever occurred to the Clipper between 12:11 and 12:12 happened instantly and permanently.

It is possible to construct a scenario that explains the loss in some manner other than hijacking. Some have even suggested that a Pacific "Bermuda Triangle" engulfed the ship, but in reality there are only five possible causes that can really explain the loss. Perhaps the most common opinion within Pan American in 1938, and one that lingers today, was that the ship, caught in a terrible storm, was torn apart or struck by lightning which caused an explosion. It is also possible that mechanical or structural failure caused the Hawaii Clipper to break up instantly; a wing may have collapsed, an engine may have torn itself from its mount and ruptured the hull. A third possibility is sabotage—a timed explosive device might have been placed aboard the ship. Some people associated with Pan Am in the 1930s believe the Clipper was shot down by marauding Japanese fighters. The last possibility is that the Clipper was taken over physically—hijacked.

The first four explanations, when explored, distort known facts and do not fit with what we really know about the flight and the subsequent seven-day search. Of all the explanations, violent weather most contradicts the facts surrounding the Hawaii Clipper's last minute. The weather the Clipper encountered out of Guam is perhaps better known than any other aspect of the entire flight. McCarty, Guam, and Panay all made regular half-hour radio checks and none reported anything more severe than scattered showers and moderate headwinds. McCarty's noon report confirms this. The thunderstorm, the only weather in the area that could have threatened the Clipper, was still centered near the Philippine coast, several hundred miles from the Hawaii Clipper. It is conceivable that the Clipper was struck by a freak bolt of lightning, disabling the radio, and that Terletsky continued on to Manila, only to strike a mountain while flying over land. It is also possible that a bolt of lightning caused an internal explosion at 12:11. But when examined, none of these explanations fits with what we know.

The Martin Clippers, in addition to carrying two main radios and eighty pounds of repair equipment—everything from friction tape to spare tubes—also carried a small emergency radio and a trailing antenna. At its last reported position the Hawaii Clipper was still over two hours from the Philippine coast. McCarty, an experienced radio officer, had more than enough time and spare parts to repair damaged equipment or set up the emergency radio before reaching the coast. This is why Panay became concerned about the Clipper's silence after the first hour: any problem with the radio should have been repaired in that time.

But suppose the radio was beyond repair for some extraordinary reason and the Clipper continued on to the Philippines where it struck a mountain, a possibility strongly considered by the board of inquiry. Between the Clipper's noon position and Manila there was not one mountain of sufficient height to have threatened the safety of the ship. The highest mountain on the Clipper's course to Manila is just over 6,400 feet, nearly 3,000 feet less than the ship's normal cruising altitude. A higher mountain, lying about 50 miles south of the Clipper's course, rises to 8,077 feet—still at least 1,000 feet below the normal cruising altitude. So only the most ill-fated circumstances could have led the Hawaii Clipper into the side of a Philippine mountain. First, all three of the Clipper's radios and/or its main and emergency antennas would have had to be damaged beyond repair—something that never happened before or after to the flying boats. Then, three to four hours later, in partly cloudy weather, the Clipper would have had to wander far off course and drop several thousand feet before it struck a mountain.

But suppose one of these forces overtook the boat: that the Clipper hit a mountain, that lightning caused an explosion, or that a freak gale ripped the hull to shreds. If the Clipper had been torn apart by one of these forces then the mystery is

absurdly compounded by the fact that the navy—after one of
the longest and most complete searches it had ever mounted—
did not find any trace of the ship on land or at sea.

The only clue to the Hawaii Clipper in July 1938 was a
false lead. After the *Meigs'* oil samples were returned to the
United States and run through a variety of tests, both Pan
American and the navy concluded beyond any doubt that the
oil was not of the type used in the trans-Pacific Clippers. It
was bilge oil. Nothing—not luggage, clothing, scraps of paper,
blankets, not even an oil slick was found. The Hawaii Clipper
vanished without explanation.

Mechanical or structural failure also serves as poor explanation of the disaster. The Hawaii Clipper was a relatively
new aircraft, just over two years old but not so new as to have
some still undiscovered deficiencies. The engines and propellers were all nearly new and the crew was reported to have
been in good spirits at each island along the route. No one
among the Hawaii Clipper's crew or on the ground reported
any unusual mechanical problems on this flight. So from all
firsthand accounts the Hawaii Clipper flew in better than
average weather and was in serviceable condition.

Beyond all of this the Martin Clippers were rugged
airplanes. In all published accounts and first hand reports by
former PAA personnel, the Clippers, though relatively slow,
plodding aircraft, were invariably described as heavy, comfortable, strong and well made. Still, let's assume the worst and
suppose that some failure brought the Clipper down after
radio contact was lost. In the event of a minor problem the
Clipper could have landed at sea and awaited rescue. This
obviously did not occur. A cataclysmic structural failure such
as a collapsed wing strut would have torn the Clipper apart.
Cruising at 9,100 feet with approximately 1,000 gallons of
unburned fuel aboard, the Clipper, had it encountered a
massive structural or mechanic problem, would have scattered

wreckage over a wide area. Again, something should have been discovered by the *Meigs*.

A lot can be learned from the Samoan Clipper and Amelia Earhart disasters and applied to the Hawaii Clipper. The exact position of Ed Musick at the moment the Samoan Clipper exploded is not known, though the Pan American board of inquiry believed he was flying between 7,000 and 10,000 feet. The Hawaii Clipper was flying at a similar altitude and Pan American knew its exact position. After a two-day search for Musick's flying boat, the *Avocet* found various debris—clothing, paper, bits of the Samoan Clipper, and a large gas and oil slick. Identification was positive.

An explosion or structural failure in the Hawaii Clipper would have resulted in destruction virtually identical to that of the Samoan Clipper. But in the case of the Hawaii Clipper, flying at 9,100 feet, the navy knew its exact position and still was unable to find wreckage anywhere. It was not possible for a twenty-six-ton flying boat to explode or tear itself apart and knife into the ocean without leaving a trace. On the other hand, the reason the navy did *not* find Amelia Earhart was that it did not know her position; thus a search for her was really hopeless from the beginning. Also, Earhart's fuel tanks were empty and when she crashed, the aircraft probably slipped into the sea without a wreckage-scattering explosion.

For the same reason, lack of debris, it is not likely that an explosive device was placed aboard the Clipper as suggested by the U.S. Marine in the Portland FBI report.

One of the most persistent rumors surrounding the Hawaii Clipper is that it was shot or forced down by a squadron of Japanese fighters. Marjorie Kennedy heard this story shortly after her husband disappeared but she dismissed the idea. As time passed, though, Mrs. Kennedy came to feel more and more that this may have been the fate of her husband.

Yet, if the Clipper had been fired upon or forced down, McCarty would have had time to signal a Mayday. He did not. And even supposing the radio failed and some time later, thirty minutes or so, Japanese fighters encountered the Clipper and shot it down, wreckage should have been found. There is still another underlying factor that makes this as unlikely an explanation as the weather. In 1938, without radar, it would have been extremely difficult to rendezvous with the Hawaii Clipper as it raced in and out of rain squalls. A plan to stop the Hawaii Clipper by fighter action would have depended more on luck than skill, and probably would have failed.

The Hawaii Clipper did not fly into a typhoon or a swarm of Japanese fighters; instead, it flew into a web of Pacific politics, a force more powerful than any aboard realized. Though hijacking cannot be conclusively proven without a confession or demonstrable evidence, once the pieces of the political puzzle are assembled and combined with the physical facts surrounding the loss, hijacking is the most credible explanation of the Clipper's fate. Even the Hawaii Clipper's accident report leaves open this possibility:

> . . . The document reveals that no authentic trace of the airplane ever has been found and that, as a result, those who investigated its disappearance are unable to ascribe any probable cause for the disaster that is presumed to have overtaken the big flying boat. Pending the discovery of some concrete evidence as to the fate of the Hawaii Clipper, the investigation remains in an open status. . .
> The Board, therefore, respectfully submits this report with the thought that additional evidence may yet be discovered and the investigation completed at that time.

With the perspective of time there may, indeed, be new facts about the events that surrounded the loss of the Hawaii Clipper. Japan, specifically the Imperial navy, had a proven track record, the opportunity and two very strong motives to attempt this theft.

The confirmed sabotage of the radio direction finder on the day of the China Clipper's maiden flight, along with numerous editorials protesting all the trans-Pacific flights, clearly demonstrates that Japan was willing to go some distance to disrupt the route. The question is: How far would Japan go? In light of Japan's concurrent actions—sabotage, the protests, the excessive force used at Shanghai and Nanking—hijacking is not at all preposterous. Indeed, it seems to follow the course of Japanese policy. It is the ultimate conclusion to the forces that had been building for years.

The only opportunity Japan had to hijack the Hawaii Clipper was out of Guam. In the midst of the Japanese Mandates, Guam was the one vulnerable point along the Pacific line. It would have been virtually impossible to have tampered with the flights at any other base. By late 1938, security had been tightened at Alameda so that it was no longer possible for casual visitors to enter the Pan Am base. Access to the Clipper at Pearl Harbor would also have been difficult since the facilities were associated with the naval base. Japanese saboteurs, attempting to disrupt the flight at Midway or Wake, most certainly would have been spotted when they tried to land on the small atolls. Though it was possible for Japanese agents to gain access to the Clippers at Manila, Guam was the first and best point along the route to meet the westbound Hawaii Clipper. Saipan, the main headquarters for the Imperial navy, was but one hundred miles to the north of Sumay. Based on the report from the Federal Bureau of Investigation, there is good reason to believe that Japanese naval officers had been secretly landing on the eastern shore of Guam as early as late 1935 for purposes of espionage.

The time of the day, 12:11 P.M., when the Hawaii Clipper disappeared, is also significant. The Clipper had just passed the point of no return, the sun was still high, and there was plenty of time to make Koror before dark. But even more to the point, Japanese hijackers would have been assured that all of the passengers would be in the lounge eating lunch at that moment. This would have simplified the takeover.

Flight 229 was doomed for two compelling reasons. Unquestionably, the primary motive was to stop Wah Sun Choy's millions from reaching Chungking. The second motive, more complex, explains why the Hawaii Clipper may have been hijacked rather than destroyed by an explosive device.

At the time of the Hawaii Clipper's last flight, the Emily flying boat was into its second month of design. The Emily's initial design was completed sometime in late August 1938. In order for the Imperial navy to assure itself of every possible engineering advantage in the Emily, knowledge of the Martin Clipper's basic design was almost mandatory. Because the Emily's design period overlapped the loss of the Hawaii Clipper and because of certain engineering similarities, a hijacking rather than the destruction of the Hawaii Clipper makes sense.

Though the Emily did not resemble the Martin as closely as the Mavis paralleled the S-42, the Emily shared some important features with the Martin. The profile of the Emily was a close approximation of the Martin. Like the Martin engineers, Kawanishi employed four radial cooled engines in the Emily; both aircraft were high-wing, cantilevered-type monoplanes; both were constructed with a straight taper on the leading and trailing edges of the wings; and both were all metal with fabric covering only on the control surfaces. The hulls of the two boats were similar, both having flat sides and relatively long noses. Primarily intended for the military, the Emily was slightly larger and a good deal more powerful than the Martin. A few commercial models of the Emily were constructed and, like the Martin, they had two storage areas, one in the bow and the other in the tail. The Emily's galley was identically placed, just to the rear of the crew's forward quarters. The passenger compartments were found amidships as well. Though this passenger configuration was not unique to the Martins, it is something that could have been constructed differently and when included with the other design parallels, it calls into question the source and originality of the Emily's design.

Kawanishi put the Emily through its first sea trials in January 1941. Immediately, the hull proved flawed. While taxiing, spray flooded the bridge and engines. When the flying boat approached take-off speed it began hopping wildly on the water, and in a few cases, capsized. In time, these problems were corrected, primarily by increasing the depth of the hull by two feet and raising the height of the tail. The fuller body was one of the main structural differences between the Emily and the Martin and this increase in hull depth may explain why the two boats did not share more similar bodies. Still, overall dimensions of the two boats were close: the Emily's wingspan was just over 124 feet, the Martin's 130 feet; the Emily's body was a bit longer, 92 feet, with the Martin measuring 90 feet. The largest discrepancy between the two was in their heights: the Emily's tail reached 30 feet, the Martin's only 24 feet.

By 1938, Japan had created some truly fine aircraft, but they were still tied to foreign design in many areas. And, with the exceptions of the Mavis and Emily, the Japanese had not proven themselves especially gifted in the design of long-range, four-engined aircraft. Undoubtedly, the post-sea trial version of the Emily was different from its original 1938 specifications to some unknown degree. Since Kawanishi's records concerning the construction of the Emily and Mavis were burned after World War II, it is impossible to determine exactly to what extent Japan relied on Pan American's flying boats for their designs. It is known, though, that the Imperial navy supplied Kawanishi with exacting specifications for the Emily. The Mavis and the S-42 are a good match; the differences between the Emily and Martin make it more difficult to reach a final conclusion. But when the changes from the sea trials are considered along with the Japanese input into the design and the worldwide improvement in aeronautical technology between 1938 and 1941, the differences between the Emily and the Martin do not seem to be very great. In 1938, the Martin Clippers were the finest flying boats in the world, even though they were on the edge of obsolescence. The Martin design would have been a good place for Kawanishi to begin the design of the Emily.

On the one hand, the Emily was superior enough to the Martin to show that some of the Emily was the product of an original Japanese design. Still, this must be mitigated by at least two remarkable coincidences: the July 1938 disappearance of the Hawaii Clipper and the design period of the Emily during that same summer. This, along with their similar sizes, identical interior floor plans, and many overlapping engineering features, all strongly suggest that the Martin Clippers played a developmental role in the Emily's design.

In the broad picture, Choy's millions would not have altered the course of the war, but this was not how Japan saw such attempts to aid the Nationalists. The Imperial army, constantly frustrated by a war that seemed to have no end, had become frenzied in its search for victory in the summer of 1938. Anything that supported the Nationalists, no matter how slight, was seen as a threat to Japanese victory. So when the opportunity—necessity—arose to impede the flow of more aid to Chungking, the attack on Flight 229 was simply a matter of combining purposes: stop Choy and take the Hawaii Clipper.

By all appearances, it would seem that Japan gambled desperately with this operation. If the plan had failed or if it had been discovered, it would seem that Japan was risking a major confrontation with the United States. Actually, the risk was very slight. The Imperial army and navy took many similar chances before and after the disappearance of the Hawaii Clipper, eliciting nothing more than mild protests from the United States. In Shanghai, Nanking, and in dozens of smaller skirmishes the Japanese army demonstrated that it would kill any number of civilians to bring an end to the war without fear of American reaction. In the course of these battles, American property was destroyed, Americans were beaten, some were killed. In the course of the fighting around Nanking, the Imperial navy—something of a maverick in the Japanese military establishment—purposefully bombed and sunk the U.S.S. *Panay*, an American gunboat, in December 1937. Two sailors were killed and fifty wounded, some seriously. Even this act of defiance and direct aggression produced little more than a protest and request for an apology from Roosevelt. Clearly, the Japanese would have risked little in a hijack, certainly not war.

Shortly after the disappearance of the Hawaii Clipper, Japan actually proved that it was willing to openly attack a commercial airliner and kill innocent civilian passengers to help end the war. In August 1938, a CNAC Douglas passenger liner, piloted by an American, made a regularly scheduled run from Hong Kong to Chungking. Originally listed as a passenger on this flight, Dr. Fun So, an important and highly influential former Chinese finance minister, cancelled his reservations at the last minute. But two other bankers, Hsu Sing-loh of the National Commercial Savings Bank and Hu

Pei-kong, manager of the Bank of Communications, did make the flight.

Just forty miles out of Hong Kong, the pilot radioed Hong Kong, "Japanese planes following us." Within seconds the liner was riddled with machine-gun fire. Pilot H. L. Woods climbed into a cloudbank but to no avail. The fighters followed him and the mortally wounded twin-engined Douglas crashed into the Pearl River near Wangmoon. Some of the passengers who escaped the sinking aircraft were machine-gunned as they swam to shore. Two days after the CNAC Douglas went down, the gunboat U.S.S. *Mindanao* rescued the pilot, the co-pilot and three passengers. At the bottom of the Pearl River lay the bullet-riddled bodies of fourteen civilian passengers.

A small report of this incident was buried in *The New York Times*. Stanley Hornbeck and Ambassador Joseph Grew, outraged by the attack, demanded an apology. But, as in the past, Japan refused to capitulate, saying they were justified in shooting down the passenger air liner. So, just weeks after the Hawaii Clipper vanished, Japan demonstrated to the world that anything, even an action as warlike as attacking the airline of a neutral country, was worth stemming the flood of important financiers to Chungking.

If, as seems likely, the Hawaii Clipper was hijacked, then its loss, within the context of Pacific politics, was inevitable and was just one of the many hostile incidents directed against Pan American, CNAC, the U.S. navy, and American citizens.

Because of the loss of the CNAC liner in August 1938, Trippe permanently closed the line to Chungking and for the first time since the beginning of the war, the Nationalist capital was without commercial air transportation. Along with the expanding war and the loss of the Hawaii Clipper, this caused Trippe to reevaluate the trans-Pacific flights. In Octo-

ber, Trippe met with Rear Admiral Arthur Cook to inform
the navy that Pan American was losing heavily in the Pacific
and that he would have to close the route to China. Cook
wanted to keep the trans-Pacific line open and wrote a long
letter to the secretary of the navy asking for higher mail
subsidies for the route:

In the first place, Pan American's activities from the
beginning have been of tremendous value to the Navy.
Its pioneering work in equipment, methods,
development of routes, establishment of aids to
seaplane operation and opening up of foreign territory
to air activity, have done far more than can be
measured in concrete terms to assist Naval Aviation in
its own development and progress. For this reason and
because of Pan American's continuing close
cooperation with the Navy and its eagerness, always
making available to the Navy its facilities, information
and assistance, its problems merit all practicable
support from the Navy Department at all times.

Considering specifically the Pan American route
between Pearl Harbor and Manila, the value to
National Defense of its continued operation is
unquestionably very high. This route constitutes our
major source of information as to air operating
conditions in this entire and highly important strategic
area and in war emergency the information as to
aerological matters and methods and necessary
facilities in this area that Pan American is contributing
and should continue to contribute, will be of immense
value.

Furthermore, the specific question as to rates over
the Pearl Harbor-Manila route is intimately associated
with the whole Pan American development in the

Pacific. Inability to continue this line at a reasonable profit will jeopardize other Pan American developments, including the Australia route via Canton Island which is, perhaps, of even greater importance and potential value to the Navy.

In short, from every angle, the Navy's interest is directly served by the activities of Pan American Airways and National Defense will benefit out of all proportions to the cost involved if Pan American's current request for easement on its Pearl Harbor-Manila problem is favorably considered.

Predictably, Trippe was granted higher mail subsidies, and not only did Pan American remain in the Pacific but it actually expanded its routes. In 1939, eleven Boeing B–314's, a new generation of flying boats, were delivered to Pan American. Seven of the Boeings were put into service across the Atlantic to Great Britain and the remaining four flew the route to Auckland, New Zealand, occasionally supplementing the Martin Clippers on the flights to China.

In the summer of 1939, Pan American moved its West Coast operations from Alameda to specially built facilities at the Golden Gate Exposition in the center of San Francisco Bay on Treasure Island. Later in the summer, after a series of test flights, the line to New Zealand was officially inaugurated—via Honolulu, Canton Island, and Noumea, New Caledonia.

But this was not accomplished without a serious, nearly violent confrontation between the United States and Great Britain. In May 1939, the *North Haven* and a U.S. navy sub chaser anchored off Canton Island and began shuttling supplies ashore for the new Pan American base. Later in the day, a British cruiser blocked the two American ships and demanded that they leave the island. The *North Haven* refused to comply and at the end of the day the cruiser withdrew, leaving the island in possession of Pan American.

From 1939 to December 7, 1941, the navy continued to lobby for appropriations to fortify the Pacific islands, but through the years Congress steadfastly refused to allocate funds. Not until the summer of 1941 did the military finally supplement Pan American's facilities. Crude landing strips were cut on Midway and Wake, the Army Corps of Engineers constructed a five thousand-foot runway on Canton, and some light aeronautical facilities were built on Palmyra and Johnston Islands south of Hawaii. Other than this, the state of aeronautical development in the Pacific was little different from 1935.

During the Japanese raid of December 7 and 8, all of Pan Am's Pacific bases suffered heavy losses. The Philippine Clipper was riddled with machine-gun fire at Wake but escaped serious damage. The new Hong Kong Clipper was destroyed by Japanese bombs at Hong Kong. Canton Island was bombed as was the deserted runway at Howland. In all, nine Pan American personnel were killed, eighty-one captured, and millions of dollars of equipment destroyed. As predicted for years prior to 1941, the initial battlefront followed the Pan American trans-Pacific line—Manila, Guam, and Wake fell shortly after December 7 and the pivotal battle of the Pacific war raged around Midway in the spring of 1942.

After the declaration of war, all of Pan Am's Clippers were pressed into naval service. The China and Philippine Clippers flew military personnel and medical supplies between San Francisco and Pearl Harbor almost daily while the Boeing Clippers continued their runs to New Zealand until the end of the war. On January 21, 1943, the Philippine Clipper crashed into the side of a mountain north of San Francisco during a fierce storm. A few months later, the China Clipper, now beginning to show its age, was returned to Pan

American and put on a regular passenger run across the Atlantic from Miami through the Caribbean to Leopoldville in the Belgian Congo. After nearly ten years of service, the China Clipper made its last flight on January 8, 1945.

Designated Flight 161, the China Clipper left Miami at 6:08 A.M., and at 8:00 P.M. it banked into its final approach over the bay at Port of Spain, Trinidad. On the approach, the pilot, Leonard Cramer, became confused by the glassy water and struck the bay sooner than anticipated at a nose-down angle, tearing the Clipper in half. Nine crew members and fourteen passengers were killed instantly while the seven survivors were tossed free of the sinking ship.

On April 8, 1946, the Pacific Clipper, a B–314, made Pan American's last seaplane flight. After the war, Pan American continued its association with CNAC until the communist takeover, and, for a short time in 1948, CNAC even made twice-weekly flights to San Francisco from Shanghai.

The navy temporarily occupied Micronesia after the War, but in 1947, jurisdiction of the islands was transferred to the Department of the Interior when the United States under an agreement with the United Nations became the permanent administrating authority of the archipelago. The army abandoned Canton in 1945 and the island once again served as a stop for several South Pacific airlines until improved technology rendered the base unnecessary as a refueling point. In 1970, Canton became a down-range tracking station for the United States Air Force. The atoll is still under joint Anglo-American jurisdiction and will remain so until 1990, when the island's sovereignty will once again be subject to negotiation.

The airlines skipped Midway as a refueling base after the war and it is now a naval installation servicing Polaris submarines. Wake continued to be useful as a refueling base into the jet age until it too was skipped by the new long-range jets in the late 1960s.

Ironically, after the war the United States navy commandeered one of the three surviving Emilys and flew it to Norfolk, Virginia to run it through diagnostic testing. Through the war the Emily was highly regarded by American pilots and generally considered superior to any American flying boat. The navy wanted to know why the Emily had performed so well. After months of testing, the navy was disappointed to discover that the Emily was not nearly as advanced as had been thought. The Emily had impressed American fighter pilots because Kawanishi fitted the flying boat with oversized engines. Generating 7,500 horsepower compared to the Martin's 3,800, it was easy to see why the Emily had dazzled American pilots. Predictably, other than that, the navy learned little from the Emily.

In April 1979, this Emily was crated and shipped to the Tokyo Museum of Maritime Science.

Sources and Acknowledgments

DOCUMENTS from various federal agencies make up the backbone of *China Clipper*. The bulk of the information concerning the Navy's interest in Pacific commercial aviation, the conversations of Juan Trippe and State Department officials, Billy Mitchell's report, and the like were discovered in the following divisions of the National Archives: Record Group 72 holds documents relating to the navy's Bureau of Aeronautics; Record Group 59 contains correspondence from the secretary of state; material on natural resources and territorial matters such as William Miller's South Pacific voyage is held in Record Group 126; Record Group 80 contains the general files of the navy; Record Group 38 represents documents from the chief of naval operations, including reports from the Office of Naval Intelligence.

All of the data concerning the Japanese espionage ring on

Saipan were found in a report from the Federal Bureau of Investigation, as were the reports of suspected sabotage in the spring and summer of 1938. This information was obtained through the Freedom of Information Act.

The official accident report of the Hawaii Clipper was supplied by the National Transportation Safety Board; the Department of the Interior contributed some data about Micronesia. The Library of Congress and the Smithsonian Institution's Aeronautical Museum contain files on the Martin Clippers.

After government documents, books were the most valuable source of documentation. Literally hundreds of books were consulted but the most important were the following. Information about the general state of commercial aviation in the 1930s was found in *The Aviation Business from Kitty Hawk to Wall Street*, by Elizabeth Freudenthal; *Airways Abroad*, by Henry Ladd Smith; *International Airways*, by Alberta Worthington; *International Air Transportation and National Policy*, by Oliver James Lissitzyn; *Wings Around the World*, by Burr Leyson; and *Struggle for Airways in Latin America*, by William Burden. Data about Pan American and its flying boats were discovered in *From Crate to Clipper, Winged Highway,* and *Skyway to Asia*, all by William Grooch; *The Dream of Eagles*, by Ralph O'Neill; *The Story of the Winged-S*, by Igor Sikorsky; *Empire of the Air*, by Matthew Josephson; *Seawings*, by Edward Jablonski; *Global Mission*, by General Henry H. Arnold; *Wings Over Wake*, by Dorothy Kaucher; and *Flying Boats Since 1910*, by Kenneth Munson. Some of the books that supplied historical background on the Pacific are *The Fight for the Pacific*, by M.J. Gayn; *The Memoirs of Cordell Hull*, by Cordell Hull; *The United States in World Affairs: 1931–1940*, by the Department of State; *Japan's Pacific Mandate*, by Paul Clyde; *Ten Years in Japan*, by Joseph Grew; and *The Panay Incident:*

Prelude to War, by Manny Koginos. Three books about Amelia Earhart—*Winged Legend*, by John Burke; *Amelia Earhart Lives*, by Joe Klass; and *The Search for Amelia Earhart*, by Fred Goerner—contributed information about both Earhart and the politics of the Pacific in the 1930s. Finally, *Zero Fighter* by Martin Caidin; *Jane's All the World's Aircraft, Aircraft Profile: Mavis and Emily*, by M.C. Richards, *Combat Aircraft of the World*, edited by W.R. Taylor, and *Warplanes of the Axis*, by D. Cooke supplied background information about Japanese aeronautical engineering and/or details about the Mavis and Emily flying boats.

Literally thousands of magazine articles published between 1934 and 1941 examined every aspect of the Clippers and the more public aspects of the trans-Pacific line. The following magazines not only contributed facts but communicated the excitement surrounding the flying boats and Pan American in the 1930s. *Fortune* published several excellent articles about the organization and financing of Pan Am; *Time* and *Newsweek* contributed news reports; *Life, The Nation, The New Republic, National Geographic, Pan Pacific Magazine, Asia, Aero Digest, Geographical Review, Foreign Affairs, Saturday Evening Post, Business Week, Travel*, and *Mid Pacific Magazine* provided insights from their specific editorial policies. An article about the Emily was found in a recent copy of *Air Progress*; a modern issue of the *Journal of the Aviation Historical Society* contains several articles about the Martin flying boats; and a recent copy of *Pacific Historical Review* published a valuable article about the Pacific Mandates.

Daily newspaper accounts of the events in the Far East, and of building and flying the Clippers, sketched an outline for *Clipper*. Through the 1930s *The New York Times* carried hundreds of pieces about Pan American. The San Francisco

Examiner and *Chronicle* and the Alameda *Times-Star* contained articles with a local slant. *The Oregonian* published biographical data on Howard French; the Jersey City *Journal* contained some information about Wah Sun Choy; and the *Washington Post* published several articles about Earl McKinley, Fred Meier, and Wah Sun Choy. The *Japan Times* and Osaka *Mainichi* were sources for the Japanese side of some events.

Two graduate theses helped construct a bibliography. *The Young Officers Movement in Japan, ca. 1925-1937; Ideology and Actions*, by Royal Jules Wald, clarified the Japanese military's temperament in the 1930s. *United States National Defense and Trans-Pacific Commercial Air Routes 1933–1941*, by Francis Holbrook, is a scholar's view of the events in the Pacific, and also simplified locating many documents in the National Archives.

Many sources do not fall into any obvious category. The Hoover Institute at Stanford University holds all of Stanley Hornbeck's papers. The library at the University of California, Berkeley supplied virtually every magazine, newspaper, and book listed here. Martin Marietta Corporation, the succeeding company of Glenn Martin, contributed biographical information about Glenn Martin and some photographs. The Jersey City Library and the State of New Jersey helped locate some biographical information about Wah Sun Choy. Shin Meiwa Industry Company of Tokyo, the succeeding company of Kawanishi, contributed photographs and some data about the Mavis and Emily.

Obviously, Pan American World Airways furnished much of the corporate data contained in these pages. The Pan American Archives in New York are the source for much of the information about the Clippers, Juan Trippe, and part of the sabotage accounts of November 1935 and January 1936. Many of the fine photographs contained in these pages were generously donated by Pan American. At Pan American in New York James Arey, director of public relations, and Ann Whyte assisted my research. William Ferris and John Leslie helped as far as they were able. At Pan American San Francisco Willard Marsh and Louise Gray helped locate many valuable photographs.

Former Martin Clipper pilots Scotty Lewis and H.G. Gulbranson gave firsthand accounts of the Martin flying boats, told stories about their flights, and offered insights into some of the personalities in this book. John Boyle, airport manager at Pearl Harbor, Midway, Wake, Guam and Macao during the 1930s, recalled stories about the pilots and the Clippers, and explained how each of the bases operated.

Lewis Wine, a former FBI agent in Oakland in the 1930s, confirmed that he had investigated several cases of sabotage at the Pan American base in Alameda. Due to his obligation of secrecy, Mr. Wine was unable to elaborate on the investigations. The only relative or friend of the passengers and crew on the ill-fated Hawaii Clipper that could be found was Marjorie Kennedy, wife of Kenneth Kennedy. Mrs. Kennedy, now living in Denver, Colorado, helped with information about her husband and Pan Am operations at Alameda, and offered some insights into Amelia Earhart.

William Slattery, formerly of the San Francisco FBI, Jack Clark at the Alameda *Times-Star*, and Les Forden of World Airways contributed from their specific areas of expertise.

Robert and Wayne Jackson, Steve and Barbara Jones, and Tom Nadeau helped in their own way.

Howard Bray at the Fund for Investigative Journalism in Washington was one of the early supporters of this book and granted me funds that helped me complete research in New York and Washington.

Also thanks to my agents, George and Olga Wieser, and to Bill Thompson at Everest House.

More than anything or anyone Marcy Jackson sustained this work. She offered invaluable aid and generously gave more comfort than can be repaid by these words.

INDEX

Bold-face figures indicate illustrations

Corporation, and Pan Am, 92-3; breakup of, 106

United Airlines, Kennedy and, 8

United States, and Japan-China war, 5-7; and Japan, 28, 30, 32-3, 63-5, 124, 151-2, 175-6, 201-2, 205, *see also* Joint Board; territorial claims of, 24-5, 170-1, 175-6, *see also names of* places; and World War I, 27; and trans-oceanic flights, 57-8, 66, *see also* trans-Atlantic, trans-Pacific, and Pan American Airways; and aviation subsidies, 123, 134; and Earhart, 152-3; *see also* under Pacific, *various U.S. departments, and items throughout*

U.S. Army, and Pacific mission, 31-2

U.S. Commerce Department, and South Pacific cruises, 80

U.S. Congress, xii, 65; and Pacific, 78, 205; and Pan Am mail contract, 107

U.S. Interior Department, and atolls, 151-2, 171-2, 175-7; and Micronesia, 206

U.S. Marine, letter from, 55-6

U.S. Marines, and Hawaii Clipper, 195

U.S. Navy, xii, xiv; and Japan, 26, 30, 63-5, 116, 124-5, 174, 202; and Pan Am, 34, 71-4, 77-8, 111, 117, 124-5, 169-70, 203-5; and Wake, 75-8, 134; and South Pacific, 80, 151, 169-70, 177, 205; and Canton Island, 171, 177; and Hawaii Clipper, 188-9, 194-5; and Earhart, 195; and Micronesia, 206; and "Emily," 207

U.S. Office of Naval Intelligence, 64-5; espionage reports from, 126; to Trippe, 125; and Koror, 187

U.S. Post Office, and Pan Am, 34-5, 49, 90-2, 94, 103, 106; and aviation subsidies, 34-6, 40, 89-90, 103, 105-6; and mail contracts, 88-91, 103-4, 106

U.S. Senate, and mail contracts, 88-90, 94, 103, *see also* Black Committee; Naval Affairs Committee of, and Guam, 29

U.S. State Department, xii; Division of Far Eastern affairs of, 66, 76; and

Pacific, 62, 73, 78, 116; Trippe and Pan Am and, 68-9, 94, 103, 121-3; and Wake Island, 76-7; and Canton Island, 156, 165, 170, 177; and Koror Island, 187

U.S. Supreme Court, and Japanese, 30

U.S. War Department, Pan Am and, 35; and South Pacific cruise, 80

Vanderbilt, William, 38, 40

Van Dusen, C. A., 60-1

Von Bauer, Dr. Peter Paul, 35-6, 51

Waco Aircraft, Terletsky and, 14

Wah Sun Choy, 41; quote from, xii; and flight to China, 3-4, 6, 8, 12, 16-18, 20-1, 53-4, 56, 83-7, 130, 183-6; and war, 4, 6-7, 12, 87; background of, 6-7; and money for Nationalists, 6-7, 86-7, 179, 187, 191, 198, 200-1; at Guam, 180-2

Waikiki, Clipper passengers in, 54, 181

Wake Island, xii, xiv, 5, 197; U.S. and, 25, 30, 32, 65, 73-4, 78-9; administration of, 73, 75-8, 134, 151; supplies for, 86, 96; Hawaii Clipper at, 99, 129, 181; landing pier at, 100; lounge in hotel of, 100; base at, 108-9, 117; description of, 129; Philippine Clipper at, 205; fall of, 205; landing strip at, 205; postwar use of, 206

Walker, Mark, 21-2, 52, 83, 182, 184

Warner Brothers, xiii

Washington Naval Treaty, 29-32, 64-5, 73, 77, 119-20

weather, *see under* Pacific *and* Hawaii Clipper

West, and Sino-Japanese war, 163

West Indian Aerial Express, 51

Whangpoo River, ships in, 158-9

Whitney, Cornelius Vanderbilt, 38, 40, 93; with Trippe and Glover, 95

Whitney, John Hay, 38

Woods, H. L., 202

Woods-Humphrey, G. E., 57, 67-8

Woolworth, Frank, 38

Woosing, Japanese sailors at, 161

World War I, 25-7

MAY   1980